The Philosophy of Spirit

George Hegel

Introduction

The knowledge of Mind is the highest and hardest, just because it is the most 'concrete' of sciences. The significance of that 'absolute' commandment, Know thyself -- whether we look at it in itself or under the historical circumstances of its first utterance -- is not to promote mere self-knowledge in respect of the particular capacities, character, propensities, and foibles of the single self. The knowledge it commands means that of man's genuine reality -- of what is essentially and ultimately true and real -- of mind as the true and essential being. Equally little is it the purport of mental philosophy to teach what is called knowledge of men -- the knowledge whose aim is to detect the peculiarities, passions, and foibles of other men, and lay bare what are called the recesses of the human heart. Information of this kind is, for one thing, meaningless, unless on the assumption that we know the universal - man as man, and, that always must be, as mind. And for another, being only engaged with casual, insignificant, and untrue aspects of mental life, it fails to reach the underlying essence of them all -- the mind itself.

Pneumatology, or, as it was also called, Rational Psychology, has been already alluded to in the Introduction to the Logic as an abstract and generalizing metaphysic of the subject. Empirical (or inductive) psychology, on the other hand, deals with the 'concrete' mind: and, after the revival of the sciences, when observation and experience had been made the distinctive methods for the study of concrete reality, such psychology was worked on the same lines as other sciences. In this way it came about that the metaphysical theory was kept outside the inductive science, and so prevented from getting any concrete embodiment or detail: whilst at the same time the inductive science clung to the conventional common-sense metaphysics with its analysis into forces, various activities, etc., and rejected any attempt at a 'speculative' treatment.

The books of Aristotle on the Soul, along with his discussions on its special aspects and states, are for this reason still by far the most admirable, perhaps even the sole, work of philosophical value on this topic. The main aim of a philosophy of mind can only be to reintroduce unity of idea and principle into the theory of mind, and so reinterpret the lesson of those Aristotelian books.

Even our own sense of the mind's living unity naturally protests against any attempt to break it up into different faculties, forces, or, what comes to the same thing, activities, conceived as independent of each other. But the craving for a comprehension of the unity is still further stimulated, as we soon come across distinctions between mental freedom and mental determinism, antitheses between free psychic agency and the corporeity that lies external to it, whilst we equally note the intimate interdependence of the one upon the other. In modern times especially the phenomena of animal magnetism have given, even in experience, a lively and visible confirmation of the underlying unity of soul, and of the power of its 'ideality'. Before these facts, the rigid distinctions of practical common sense are struck with confusion; and the necessity of a 'speculative' examination with a view to the removal of difficulties is more directly forced upon the student.

The 'concrete' nature of mind involves for the observer the peculiar difficulty that the several grades and special types which develop its intelligible unity in detail are not left standing as so many separate existences confronting its more advanced aspects. It is otherwise in external nature. There, matter and movement, for example, have a manifestation all their own -- it is the solar system; and similarly the differentiae of sense-perception have a sort of earlier existence in the properties of bodies, and still more independently in the four elements. The species and grades of mental evolution, on the contrary, lose their separate existence and become factors, states, and features in the higher grades of development. As a consequence of this, a lower and more abstract aspect of mind betrays the presence in it, even to experience, of a higher grade. Under the guise of sensation, for example, we may find the very highest mental life as its modification or its embodiment. And so sensation, which is but a mere form and vehicle, may to the superficial glance seem to be the proper seat and, as it were, the source of those moral and religious principles with which it is charged; and the moral and religious principles thus modified may seem to call for treatment as species of sensation. But at the same time, when lower grades of mental life are under examination, it becomes necessary, if we desire to point to actual cases of them in experience, to direct attention to more advanced grades for which they are mere forms. In this way subjects will be treated of by anticipation which properly belong to later stages of development (e.g. in dealing with natural awaking from sleep we speak by anticipation of consciousness, or in dealing with mental derangement we must speak of intellect).

What Mind Is

From our point of view mind has for its presupposition Nature, of which it is the truth, and for that reason its absolute prius. In this its truth Nature is vanished, and mind has resulted as the 'Idea' entered on possession of itself. Here the subject and object of the Idea are one -- either is the intelligent unity, the notion. This identity is absolute negativity -- for whereas in Nature the intelligent unity has its objectivity perfect but externalized, this self-externalization has been nullified and the unity in that way been made one and the same with itself. Thus at the same time it is this identity only so far as it is a return out of nature.

For this reason the essential, but formally essential, feature of mind is Liberty: i.e. it is the notion's absolute negativity or self-identity. Considered as this formal aspect, it may withdraw itself from everything external and from its own externality, its very existence; it can thus submit to infinite pain, the negation of its individual immediacy: in other words, it can keep itself affirmative in this negativity and possess its own identity. All this is possible so long as it is considered in its abstract self-contained universality.

This universality is also its determinate sphere of being. Having a being of its own, the universal is self-particularizing, whilst it still remains self-identical. Hence the special mode of mental being is 'manifestation'. The spirit is not some one mode or meaning which finds utterance or externality only in a form distinct from itself: it does not manifest or reveal something, but its very mode and meaning is this revelation. And thus in its mere possibility mind is at the same moment an infinite, 'absolute', actuality.

Revelation, taken to mean the revelation of the abstract Idea, is an unmediated transition to Nature which comes to be. As mind is free, its manifestation is to set forth Nature as its world; but because it is reflection, it, in thus setting forth its world, at the same time presupposes the world as a nature independently existing. In the intellectual sphere to reveal is thus to create a world as its being -- a being in which the mind procures the affirmation and truth of its freedom.

The Absolute is Mind (Spirit) -- this is the supreme definition of the Absolute. To find this definition and to grasp its meaning and burden was, we may say, the ultimate purpose of all education and all philosophy: it was the point to which turned the impulse of all religion and science: and it is this impulse that must explain the history of the world. The word 'Mind' (Spirit) -- and some glimpse of its meaning -- was found at an early period: and the spirituality of God is the lesson of Christianity. It remains for philosophy in its own element of intelligible unity to get hold of what was thus given as a mental image, and what implicitly is the ultimate reality; and that problem is not genuinely, and by rational methods, solved so long as liberty and intelligible unity is not the theme and the soul of philosophy.

The development of Mind (Spirit) is in three stages:

In the form of self-relation: within it it has the ideal totality of the Idea -- i.e. it has before it all that its notion contains: its being is to be self-contained and free. This is Mind Subjective.

In the form of reality: realized, i.e. in a world produced and to be produced by it: in this world freedom presents itself under the shape of necessity. This is Mind Objective.

In that unity of mind as objectivity and of mind as ideality and concept, which essentially and actually is and for ever produces itself, mind in its absolute truth. This is Mind Absolute.

The two first parts of the doctrine of Mind embrace the finite mind. Mind is the infinite Idea, and finitude here means the disproportion between the concept and the reality -- but with the qualification that it is a shadow cast by the mind's own light -- a show or illusion which the mind implicitly imposes as a barrier to itself, in order, by its removal, actually to realize and become conscious of freedom as its very being, i.e. to be fully manifested. The several steps of this activity, on each of which, with their semblance of being, it is the function of the finite mind to linger, and through which it has to pass, are steps in its liberation. In the full truth of that liberation is given the identification of the three stages -- finding a world presupposed before us, generating a world as our own creation, and gaining freedom from it and in it. To the infinite form of this truth the show purifies itself till it becomes a consciousness of it.

A rigid application of the category of finitude by the abstract logician is chiefly seen in dealing with Mind and reason: it is held not a mere matter of strict logic, but treated also as a moral and religious concern, to adhere to the point of view of finitude, and the wish to go further is reckoned a mark of audacity, if not of insanity, of thought. Whereas in fact such a modesty of thought, as treats the finite as something altogether fixed and absolute, is the worst of virtues; and to stick to a post which has no sound ground in itself is the most unsound sort of theory. The category of finitude was at a much earlier period elucidated and explained at its place in the Logic: an elucidation which, as in logic for the more specific though still simple thought-forms of finitude, so in the rest of philosophy for the concrete forms, has merely to show that the finite is not, i.e. is not the truth, but merely a transition and an emergence to something higher. This finitude of the spheres so far examined is the dialectic that makes a thing have its cessation by another and in another: but Spirit, the intelligent unity and the implicit Eternal, is itself just the consummation of that internal act by which nullity is nullified and vanity is made vain. And so, the modesty alluded to is a retention of this vanity -- the finite -- in opposition to the true: it is itself therefore vanity. In the course of the mind's development we shall see this vanity appear as wickedness at that turning-point at which mind has reached its extreme immersion in its subjectivity and its most central contradiction.

SECTION ONE - MIND SUBJECTIVE

Mind, on the ideal stage of its development, is mind as cognitive. Cognition, however, being taken here not as a merely logical category of the Idea, but in the sense appropriate to the concrete mind.

Subjective mind is:

(A) Immediate or implicit: a soul -- the Spirit in Nature -- the object treated by Anthropology.

(B) Mediate or explicit: still as identical reflection into itself and into other things: mind in correlation or particularization: consciousness -- the object treated by the Phenomenology of Mind.

(C) Mind defining itself in itself, as an independent subject -- the object treated by Psychology.

In the Soul is the awaking of Consciousness: Consciousness sets itself up as Reason, awaking at one bound to the sense of its rationality: and this Reason by its activity emancipates itself to objectivity and the consciousness of its intelligent unity.

For an intelligible unity or principle of comprehension each modification it presents is an advance of development: and so in mind every character under which it appears is a stage in a process of specification and development, a step forward towards its goal, in order to make itself into, and to realize in itself, what it implicitly is. Each step, again, is itself such a process, and its product is that what the mind was implicitly at the beginning (and so for the observer) it is for itself -- for the special form, viz. which the mind has in that step. The ordinary method of psychology is to narrate what the mind or soul is, what happens to it, what it does. The soul is presupposed as a ready-made agent, which displays such features as its acts and utterances, from which we can learn what it is, what sort of faculties and powers it possesses -- all without being aware that the act and utterance of what the soul is really invests it with that character in our conception and makes it reach a higher stage of being than it explicitly had before.

We must, however, distinguish and keep apart from the progress here to be studied what we call education and instruction. The sphere of education is the individuals only: and its aim is to bring the universal mind to exist in them. But in the philosophic theory of mind, mind is studied as self-instruction and self-education in very essence; and its acts and utterances are stages in the process which brings it forward to itself, links it in unity with itself, and so makes it actual mind.

A. ANTHROPOLOGY. The Soul

(a) The Physical Soul
(b) The Feeling Soul
(c) The Actual Soul

Spirit (Mind) came into being as the truth of Nature. But not merely is it, as such a result, to be held the true and real first of what went before: this becoming or transition bears in the sphere of the notion the special meaning of 'free judgement'. Mind, thus come into being, means therefore that Nature in its own self realizes its untruth and sets itself aside: it means that Mind presupposes itself no longer as the universality which in corporal individuality is always self-externalized, but as a universality which in its concretion and totality is one and simple. At such a stage it is not yet mind, but soul.

The soul is no separate immaterial entity. Wherever there is Nature, the soul is its universal immaterialism, its simple 'ideal' life. Soul is the substance or 'absolute' basis of all the particularizing and individualizing of mind: it is in the soul that mind finds the material on which its character is wrought, and the soul remains the pervading, identical ideality of it all. But as it is still conceived thus abstractly, the soul is only the sleep of mind -- the passive of Aristotle, which is potentially all things.

The question of the immateriality of the soul has no interest, except where, on the one hand, matter is regarded as something true, and mind conceived as a thing, on the other. But in modern times even the physicists have found matters grow thinner in their hands: they have come upon imponderable matters, like heat, light, etc., to which they might perhaps add space and time. These 'imponderables', which have lost the property (peculiar to matter) of gravity and, in a sense, even the capacity of offering resistance, have still, however, a sensible existence and outness of part to part; whereas the 'vital' matter, which may also be found enumerated among them, not merely lacks gravity, but even every other aspect of existence which might lead us to treat it as material.

The fact is that in the Idea of Life the self-externalism of nature is implicitly at an end: subjectivity is the very substance and conception of life -- with this proviso, however, that its existence or objectivity is still at the same time forfeited to the away of self-externalism. It is otherwise with Mind. There, in the intelligible unity which exists as freedom, as absolute negativity, and not as the immediate or natural individual, the object or the reality of the intelligible unity is the unity itself; and so the self-externalism, which is the fundamental feature of matter, has been completely dissipated and transmuted into universality, or the subjective ideality of the conceptual unity. Mind is the existent truth of matter -- the truth that matter itself has no truth.

A cognate question is that of the community of soul and body. This community (interdependence) was assumed as a fact, and the only problem was how to comprehend it. The usual answer, perhaps, was to call it an incomprehensible mystery; and, indeed, if we take them to be absolutely antithetical and absolutely independent, they are as impenetrable to each other as one piece of matter to another, each being supposed to be found only in the pores of the other, i.e. where the other is not -- whence Epicurus, when attributing to the gods a residence in the pores, was consistent in not imposing on them any connection with the world. A somewhat different answer has been given by all philosophers since this relation came to be expressly discussed. Descartes, Malebranche, Spinoza, and Leibniz have all indicated God as this nexus. They meant that the finitude of soul and matter were only ideal and unreal distinctions; and, so holding, there philosophers took God, not, as so often is done, merely as another word for the incomprehensible, but rather as the sole true identity of finite mind and matter. But either this identity, as in the case of Spinoza, is too abstract, or, as in the case of Leibniz, though his Monad of monads brings things into being, it does so only by an act of judgement or choice. Hence, with Leibniz, the result is a distinction between soul and the corporeal (or material), and the identity is only like the copula of a judgement, and does not rise or develop into system, into the absolute syllogism.

The Soul is at first -

(a) In its immediate natural mode -- the natural soul, which only is.

(b) Secondly, it is a soul which feels, as individualized, enters into correlation with its immediate being, and, in the modes of that being, retains an abstract independence.

(c) Thirdly, its immediate being -- or corporeity -- is moulded into it, and with that corporeity it exists as actual soul.

(a) THE PHYSICAL SOUL

The soul universal, described, it may be, as an anima mundi, a world-soul, must not be fixed on that account as a single subject; it is rather the universal substance which has its actual truth only in individuals and single subjects. Thus, when it presents itself as a single soul, it is a single soul which is merely: its only modes are modes of natural life. These have, so to speak, behind its ideality a free existence: i.e. they are natural objects for consciousness, but objects to which the soul as such does not behave as to something external. These features rather are physical qualities of which it finds itself possessed.

i. Physical Qualities

(1) While still a 'substance' (i.e. a physical soul) the mind takes part in the general planetary life, feels the difference of climates, the changes of the seasons, and the periods of the day, etc. This life of nature for the main shows itself only in occasional strain or disturbance of mental tone.

In recent times a good deal has been said of the cosmical, sidereal, and telluric life of man. In such a sympathy with nature the animals essentially live: their specific characters and their particular phases of growth depend, in many cases completely, and always more or less, upon it. In the case of man these points of dependence lose importance, just in proportion to his civilization, and the more his whole frame of soul is based upon a sub-structure of mental freedom. The history of the world is not bound up with revolutions in the solar system, any more than the destinies of individuals with the positions of the planets.

The difference of climate has a more solid and vigorous influence. But the response to the changes of the seasons and hours of the day is found only in faint changes of mood, which come expressly to the fore only in morbid states (including insanity) and at periods when the self-conscious life suffers depression.

In nations less intellectually emancipated, which therefore live more in harmony with nature, we find amid their superstitions and aberrations of imbecility a few real cases of such sympathy, and on that foundation what seems to be marvellous prophetic vision of coming conditions and of events arising therefrom. But as mental freedom gets a deeper hold, even these few and slight susceptibilities, based upon participation in the common life of nature, disappear. Animals and plants, on the contrary, remain for ever subject to such influences.

(2) According to the concrete differences of the terrestrial globe, the general planetary life of the nature-governed mind specializes itself and breaks up into the several nature-governed minds which, on the whole, give expression to the nature of the geographical continents and constitute the diversities of race.

The contrast between the earth's poles, the land towards the north pole being more aggregated and preponderant over sea, whereas in the southern hemisphere it runs out in sharp points, widely distant from each other, introduces into the differences of continents a further modification which Treviranus (Biology, Part II) has exhibited in the case of the flora and fauna.

This diversity descends into specialities, that may be termed local minds -- shown in the outward modes of life and occupation, bodily structure and disposition, but still more in the inner tendency and capacity of the intellectual and moral character of the several peoples.

Back to the very beginnings of national history we see the several nations each possessing a persistent type of its own.

(3) The soul is further de-universalized into the individualized subject. But this subjectivity is here only considered as a differentiation and singling out of the modes which nature gives; we find it as the special temperament, talent, character, physiognomy, or other disposition and idiosyncrasy, of families or single individuals.

ii. Physical Alterations

Taking the soul as an individual, we find its diversities, as alterations in it, the one permanent subject, and as stages in its development. As they are at once physical and mental diversities, a more concrete definition or description of them would require us to anticipate an acquaintance with the formed and matured mind.

(1) The first of these is the natural lapse of the ages in man's life. He begins with Childhood -- mind wrapped up in itself. His next step is the fully developed antithesis, the strain and struggle of a universality which is still subjective (as seen in ideals, fancies, hopes, ambitions) against his immediate individuality. And that individuality marks both the world which, as it exists, fails to meet his ideal requirements, and the position of the individual himself, who is still short of independence and not fully equipped for the part he has to play (Youth). Thirdly, we see man in his true relation to his environment, recognizing the objective necessity and reasonableness of the world as he finds it -- a world no longer incomplete, but able in the work which it collectively achieves to afford the individual a place and a security for his performance. By his share in this collective work he first is really somebody, gaining an effective existence and an objective value (Manhood). Last of all comes the finishing touch to this unity with objectivity: a unity which, while on its realist side it passes into the inertia of deadening habit, on its idealist side

gains freedom from the limited interests and entanglements of the outward present (Old Age).

(2) Next we find the individual subject to a real antithesis, leading it to seek and find itself in another individual. This -- the sexual relation -- on a physical basis, shows, on its one side, subjectivity remaining in an instinctive and emotional harmony of moral life and love, and not pushing these tendencies to an extreme universal phase, in purposes political, scientific, or artistic; and on the other, shows an active half, where the individual is the vehicle of a struggle of universal and objective interests with the given conditions (both of his own existence and of that of the external world), carrying out these universal principles into a unity with the world which is his own work. The sexual tie acquires its moral and spiritual significance and function in the family.

(3) When the individuality, or self-centralized being, distinguishes itself from its mere being, this immediate judgement is the waking of the soul, which confronts its self-absorbed natural life, in the first instance, as one natural quality and state confronts another state, viz. sleep.-- The waking is not merely for the observer, or externally distinct from the sleep: it is itself the judgement (primary partition) of the individual soul -- which is self-existing only as it relates its self-existence to its mere existence, distinguishing itself from its still undifferentiated universality. The waking state includes generally all self-conscious and rational activity in which the mind realizes its own distinct self.-- Sleep is an invigoration of this activity -- not as a merely negative rest from it, but as a return back from the world of specialization, from dispersion into phases where it has grown hard and stiff -- a return into the general nature of subjectivity, which is the substance of those specialized energies and their absolute master.

The distinction between sleep and waking is one of those posers, as they may be called, which are often addressed to philosophy:-- Napoleon, for example, on a visit to the University of Pavia, put this question to the class of ideology. The characterization given in the section is abstract; it primarily treats waking merely as a natural fact, containing the mental element implicate but not yet as invested with a special being of its own. If we are to speak more concretely of this distinction (in fundamentals it remains the same), we must take the self-existence of the individual soul in its higher aspects as the Ego of consciousness and as intelligent mind. The difficulty raised anent the distinction of the two states properly arises, only when we also take into account the dreams in sleep and describe these dreams, as well as the mental representations in the sober waking consciousness under one and the same title of mental representations. Thus superficially classified as states of mental representation the two coincide, because we have lost sight of the difference; and in the case of any assignable distinction of waking consciousness, we can always return to the trivial remark that all this is nothing more than mental idea. But the concrete theory of the wakin soul in its realized being views it as consciousness and intellect: and the world of intelligent consciousness is something quite different from a picture of mere ideas and images. The latter are in the main only externally conjoined, in an unintelligent way, by the laws of the so-called Association of Ideas; though here and there of course logical principles may also be operative. But in the waking state man behaves essentially as a concrete ego, an intelligence: and because of this intelligence his sense-perception stands before him as a concrete totality of features in which each member, each point, takes up its place as at the same time determined through and with all the rest. Thus the facts embodied in his sensation are authenticated, not by his mere subjective representation and distinction of the facts as something external from the person, but by virtue of the concrete interconnection in which each part stands with all parts of this complex. The waking state is the concrete consciousness of this mutual corroboration of each single factor of its content by all the others in the picture as perceived. The consciousness of this interdependence need not be explicit and distinct. Still this general setting to all sensations is implicitly present in the concrete feeling of self.-- In order to see the difference between dreaming and waking we need only keep in view the Kantian distinction between subjectivity and objectivity of mental representation (the latter depending upon determination through categories): remembering, as already noted, that what is actually present in mind need not be therefore explicitly realized in consciousness, just as little as the exaltation of the intellectual sense to God need stand before consciousness in the shape of proofs of God's existence, although, as before explained, these proofs only serve to express the net worth and content of that feeling.

Sleep and waking are, primarily, it is true, not mere alterations, but alternating conditions (a progression in infinitum). This is their formal and negative relationship: but in it the affirmative relationship is also involved. In the self-certified existence of waking soul its mere existence is implicit as an 'ideal' factor: the features which make up its sleeping nature, where they are implicitly as in their substance, are found by the waking soul, in its own self, and, be it noted, for itself. The fact that these particulars, though as a mode of mind they are distinguished from the self- identity of our self-centred being, are yet simply contained in its simplicity, is what we call sensibility.

Sensibility (feeling) is the form of the dull stirring, the inarticulate breathing, of the spirit through its unconscious and unintelligent individuality, where every definite feature is still 'immediate' -- neither specially developed in its content nor set in distinction as objective to subject, but treated as belonging to its most special, its natural peculiarity. The content of sensation is thus limited and transient, belonging as it does to natural, immediate being -- to what is therefore qualitative and finite.

Everything is in sensation (feeling): if you will, everything that emerges in conscious intelligence and in reason has its source and origin in sensation; for source and origin just means the first immediate manner in which a thing appears. Let it not be enough to have principles and religion only in the head: they must also be in the heart, in the feeling. What we merely have in the head is in consciousness, in a general way: the facts of it are objective -- set over against consciousness, so that as it is put in me (my abstract ego) it can also be kept away and apart from me (from my concrete subjectivity). But if put in the feeling, the fact is a mode of my individuality, however crude that individuality be in such a form: it is thus treated as my very own. My own is something inseparate from the actual concrete self: and this immediate unity of the soul with its underlying self in all its definite content is just this inseparability; which, however, yet falls short of the ego of developed consciousness, and still more of the freedom of rational mind-life. It is with a quite different intensity and permanency that the will, the conscience, and the character, are our very own, than can ever be true of feeling and of the group of feelings (the heart): and this we need no philosophy to tell us. No doubt it is correct to say that above everything the heart must be good. But feeling and heart is not the form by which anything is legitimated as religious, moral, true, just, etc., and an appeal to heart and feeling either means nothing or means something bad. This should hardly need enforcing. Can any experience be more trite than that feelings and hearts are also bad, evil, godless, mean, etc.? That the heart is the source only of such feelings is stated in the words: 'From the heart proceed evil thoughts, murder, adultery, fornication, blasphemy, etc.' In such times when 'scientific' theology and philosophy make the heart and feeling the criterion of what is good, moral, and religious, it is necessary to remind them of these trite experiences; just as it is nowadays necessary to repeat that thinking is the characteristic property by which man is distinguished from the beasts, and that he has feeling in common with them.

What the sentient soul finds within it is, on one hand, the naturally immediate, as 'ideally' in it and made its own. On the other hand and conversely, what originally belongs to the central individuality (which as further deepened and enlarged is the conscious ego and free mind) gets the features of the natural corporeity, and is so felt. In this way we have two spheres of feeling. One, where what at first is a corporeal affection (e.g. of the eye or of any bodily part whatever) is made feeling (sensation) by being driven inward, memorized in the soul's self-centred part. Another, where affections originating in the mind and belonging to it, are in order to be felt, and to be as if found, invested with corporeity. Thus the mode or affection gets a place in the subject: it is felt in the soul. The detailed specification of the former branch of sensibility is seen in the system of the senses. But the other or inwardly originated modes of feeling no less necessarily systematize themselves; and their corporization, as put in the living and concretely developed natural being, works itself out, following the special character of the mental mode, in a special system of bodily organs.

Sensibility in general is the healthy fellowship of the individual mind in the life of its bodily part. The senses form the simple system of corporeity specified.

(a) The 'ideal' side of physical things breaks up into two -- because in it, as immediate and not yet subjective ideality, distinction appears as mere variety -- the senses of definite light, -- and of sound,. The 'real' aspect similarly is with its difference double:

(b) the senses of smell and taste,;

(c) the sense of solid reality, of heavy matter, of heat and shape. Around the centre of the sentient individuality these specifications arrange themselves more simply than when they are developed in the natural corporeity.

The system by which the internal sensation comes to give itself specific bodily forms would deserve to be treated in detail in a peculiar science -- a psychical physiology. Somewhat pointing to such a system is implied in the feeling of the appropriateness or inappropriateness of an immediate sensation to the persistent tone of internal sensibility (the pleasant and unpleasant): as also in the distinct parallelism which underlies the symbolical employment of sensations, e.g. of colours, tones, smells. But the most interesting side of a psychical physiology would lie in studying not the mere sympathy, but more definitely the bodily form adopted by certain mental modifications, especially the passions or emotions. We should have, for example, to explain the line of connection by which anger and courage are felt in the breast, the blood, the 'irritable' system, just as thinking and mental occupation are felt in the head, the centre of the 'sensible' system. We should want a more satisfactory explanation than hitherto of the most familar connections by which tears, and voice in general, with its varieties of language, laughter, sighs, with many other specializations lying in the line of pathognomy and physiognomy, are formed from their mental source. In physiology the viscera and the organs are treated merely as parts subservient to the animal organism; but they form at the same time a physical system for the expression of mental states, and in this way they get quite another interpretation.

Sensations, just because they are immediate and are found existing, are single and transient aspects of psychic life -- alterations in the substantiality of the soul, set in its self-centred life, with which that substance is one. But this self-centred being is not merely a formal factor of sensation: the soul is virtually a reflected totality of sensations -- it feels in itself the total substantiality which it virtually is -- it is a soul which feels.

In the usage of ordinary language, sensation and feeling are not clearly distinguished: still we do not speak of the sensation -- but of the feeling (sense) of right, of self; sentimentality (sensibility) is connected with sensation: we may therefore say sensation emphasizes rather the side of passivity-the fact that we find ourselves feeling, i.e. the immediacy of mode in feeling -- whereas feeling at the same time rather notes the fact that it is we ourselves who feel.

(b) THE FEELING SOUL - (Soul as Sentiency)

The feeling or sentient individual is the simple 'ideality' or subjective side of sensation. What it has to do, therefore, is to raise its substantiality, its merely virtual filling-up, to the character of subjectivity, to take possession of it, to realize its mastery over its own. As sentient, the soul is no longer a mere natural, but an inward, individuality: the individuality which in the merely substantial totality was only formal to it has to be liberated and made independent.

Nowhere so much as in the case of the soul (and still more of the mind) if we are to understand it, must that feature of 'ideality' be kept in view, which represents it as the negation of the real, but a negation, where the real is put past, virtually retained, although it does not exist. The feature is one with which we are familiar in regard to our mental ideas or to memory. Every individual is an infinite treasury of sensations, ideas, acquired lore, thoughts, etc.; and yet the ego is one and uncompounded, a deep featureless characterless mine, in which all this is stored up, without existing. It is only when I call to mind an idea, that I bring it out of that interior to existence before consciousness. Sometimes, in sickness, ideas and information, supposed to have been forgotten years ago, because for so long they had not been brought into consciousness, once more come to light. They were not in our possession, nor by such reproduction as occurs in sickness do they for the future come into our possession; and yet they were in us and continue to be in us still. Thus a person can never know how much of things he once learned he really has in him, should he have once forgotten them: they belong not to his actuality or subjectivity as such, but only to his implicit self. And under all the superstructure of specialized and instrumental consciousness that may subsequently be added to it, the individuality always remains this single-souled inner life. At the present stage this singleness is, primarily, to be defined as one of feeling -- as embracing the corporeal in itself: thus denying the view that this body is something material, with parts outside parts and outside the soul. Just as the number and variety of mental representations is no argument for an extended and real multeity in the ego; so the 'real' outness of parts in the body has no truth for the sentient soul. As sentient, the soul is characterized as immediate, and so as natural and corporeal: but the outness of parts and sensible multiplicity of this corporeal counts for the soul (as it counts for the intelligible unity) not as anything real, and therefore not as a barrier: the soul is this intelligible unity in existence -- the existent speculative principle. Thus in the body it is one simple, omnipresent unity. As to the representative faculty the body is but one representation, and the infinite variety of its material structure and organization is reduced to the simplicity of one definite conception: so in the sentient soul, the corporeity, and all that outness of parts to parts which belongs to it, is reduced to ideality (the truth of the natural multiplicity). The soul is virtually the totality of nature: as an individual soul it is a monad: it is itself the explicitly put totality of its particular world -- that world being included in it and filling it up; and to that world it stands but as to itself.

As individual, the soul is exclusive and always exclusive: any difference there is, it brings within itself. What is differentiated from it is as yet no external object (as in consciousness), but only the aspects of its own sentient totality, etc. In this partition (judgement) of itself it is always subject: its object is its substance, which is at the same time its predicate. This substance is still the content of its natural life, but turned into the content of the individual sensation-laden soul; yet as the soul is in that content still particular, the content is its particular world, so far as that is, in an implicit mode, included in the ideality of the subject.

By itself, this stage of mind is the stage of its darkness: its features are not developed to conscious and intelligent content: so far it is formal and only formal. It acquires a peculiar interest in cases where it is as a form and appears as a special state of mind, to which the soul, which has already advanced to consciousness and intelligence, may again sink down. But when a truer phase of mind thus exists in a more subordinate and abstract one, it implies a want of adaptation, which is disease. In the present stage we must treat, first, of the abstract psychical modifications by themselves, secondly, as morbid states of mind: the latter being only explicable by means of the former.

(a) The feeling soul in its immediacy

i. The Psychical Tie

Though the sensitive individuality is undoubtedly a monadic individual, it is, because immediate, not yet as its self, not a true subject reflected into itself, and is therefore passive. Hence the individuality of its true self is a different subject from it -- a subject which may even exist as another individual. By the self-hood of the latter it -- a substance, which is only a non-independent predicate -- is then set in vibration and controlled without the least resistance on its part. This other subject by which it is so controlled may be called its genius.

In the ordinary course of nature this is the condition of the child in its mother's womb:-- a condition neither merely bodily nor merely mental, but psychical -- a correlation of soul to soul. Here are two individuals, yet in undivided psychic unity: the one as yet no self, as yet nothing impenetrable, incapable of resistance: the other is its actuating subject, the single self of the two. The mother is the genius of the child; for by genius we commonly mean the total mental self-hood, as it has existence of its own, and constitutes the subjective substantiality of some one else who is only externally treated as an individual and has only a nominal independence. The underlying essence of the genius is the sum total of existence, of life, and of character, not as a mere possibility, or capacity, or virtuality, but as efficiency and realized activity, as concrete subjectivity.

If we look only to the spatial and material aspects of the child's existence as an embryo in its special integuments, and as connected with the mother by means of umbilical cord, placenta, etc., all that is presented to the senses and reflection are certain anatomical and physiological facts -- externalities and instrumentalities in the sensible and material which are insignificant as regards the main point, the psychical relationship. What ought to be noted as regards this psychical tie are not merely the striking effects communicated to and stamped upon the child by violent emotions, injuries, etc., of the mother, but the whole psychical judgement (partition) of the underlying nature, by which the female (like the monocotyledons among vegetables) can suffer disruption in twain, so that the child has not merely got communicated to it, but has originally received morbid dispositions as well as other predispositions of shape, temper, character, talent, idiosyncrasies, etc.

Sporadic examples and traces of this magic tie appear elsewhere in the range of self-possessed conscious life, say between friends, especially female friends with delicate nerves (a tie which may go so far as to show 'magnetic' phenomena), between husband and wife and between members of the same family.

The total sensitivity has its self here in a separate subjectivity, which, in the case cited of this sentient life in the ordinary course of nature, is visibly present as another and a different individual. But this sensitive totality is meant to elevate its selfhood out of itself to subjectivity in one and the same individual: which is then its indwelling consciousness, self-possessed, intelligent, and reasonable. For such a consciousness the merely sentient life serves as an underlying and only implicitly existent material; and the self-possessed subjectivity is the rational, self-conscious, controlling genius thereof. But this sensitive nucleus includes not merely the purely unconscious, congenital disposition and temperament, but within its enveloping simplicity it acquires and retains also (in habit, as to which see later) all further ties and essential relationships, fortunes, principles-everything in short belonging to the character, and in whose elaboration self-conscious activity has most effectively participated. The sensitivity is thus a soul in which the whole mental life is condensed. The total individual under this concentrated aspect is distinct from the existing and actual play of his consciousness, his secular ideas, developed interests, inclinations, etc. As contrasted with this looser aggregate of means and methods the more intensive form of individuality is termed the genius, whose decision is ultimate whatever may be the show of reasons, intentions, means, of which the more public consciousness is so liberal. This concentrated individuality also reveals itself under the aspect of what is called the heart and soul of feeling. A man is said to be heartless and unfeeling when he looks at things with self-possession and acts according to his permanent purposes, be they great substantial aims or petty and unjust interests: a good-hearted man, on the other hand, means rather one who is at the mercy of his individual sentiment, even when it is of narrow range and is wholly made up of particularities. Of such good nature or goodness of heart it may be said that it is less the genius itself than the indulgere genio.

ii. Rapport

The sensitive life, when it becomes a form or state of the self-conscious, educated, self-possessed human being is a disease. The individual in such a morbid state stands in direct contact with the concrete contents of his own self, whilst he keeps his self-possessed consciousness of self and of the causal order of things apart as a distinct state of mind. This morbid condition is seen in magnetic somnambulism and cognate states.

In this summary encyclopaedic account it is impossible to supply a demonstration of what the paragraph states as the nature of the remarkable condition produced chiefly by animal magnetism -- to show, in other words, that it is in harmony with the facts. To that end the phenomena, so complex in their nature and so very different one from another, would have first of all to be brought under their general points of view. The facts, it might seem, first of all call for verification. But such a verification would, it must be added, be superfluous for those on whose account it was called for: for they facilitate the inquiry for themselves by declaring the narratives -- infinitely numerous though they be and accredited by the education and character of the witnesses -- to be mere deception and imposture. The a priori conceptions of these inquirers are so rooted that no testimony can avail against them, and they have even denied what they have seen with their own eyes. In order to believe in this department even what one's own eyes have seen and still more to understand it, the first requisite is not to be in bondage to the hard and fast categories of the practical intellect. The chief points on which the discussion turns may here be given:

(a) To the concrete existence of the individual belongs the aggregate of his fundamental interests, both the essential and the particular empirical ties which connect him with other men and the world at large. This totality forms his actuality, in the sense that it lies in fact immanent in him; it has already been called his genius. This genius is not the free mind which wills and thinks: the form of sensitivity, in which the individual here appears innnersed, is, on the contrary, a surrender of his self-possessed intelligent existence. The first conclusion to which these considerations lead, with reference to the contents of consciousness in the somnambulist stage, is that it is only the range of his individually moulded world (of his private interests and narrow relationships) which appear there. Scientific theories and philosophic conceptions or general truths require a different soil -- require an intelligence which has risen out of the inarticulate mass of mere sensitivity to free consciousness. It is foolish therefore to expect revelations about the higher ideas from the somnambulist state.

(b) Where a human being's senses and intellect are sound, he is fully and intelligently alive to that reality of his which gives concrete filling to his individuality: but he is awake to it in the form of interconnection between himself and the features of that reality conceived as an external and a separate world, and he is aware that this world is in itself also a complex of interconnections of a practically intelligible kind. In his subjective ideas and plans he has also before him this causally connected scheme of things he calls his world and the series of means which bring his ideas and his purposes into adjustment with the objective existences, which are also means and ends to each other. At the same time, this world which is outside him has its threads in him to such a degree that it is these threads which make him what he really is: he too would become extinct if these externalities were to disappear, unless by the aid of religion, subjective reason, and character, he is in a remarkable degree self-supporting and independent of them. But, then, in the latter case he is less susceptible of the psychical state here spoken of.-- As an illustration of that identity with the surroundings may be noted the effect produced by the death of beloved relatives, friends, etc. on those left behind, so that the one dies or pines away with the loss of the other. (Thus Cato, after the downfall of the Roman republic, could live no longer: his inner reality was neither wider nor higher than it.) Compare home-sickness, and the like.

(c) But when all that occupies the waking consciousness, the world outside it and its relationship to that world, is under a veil, and the soul is thus sunk in sleep (in magnetic sleep, in catalepsy, and other diseases, for example, those connected with female development, or at the approach of death, etc.), then that immanent actuality of the individual remains the same substantial total as before, but now as a purely sensitive life with an inward vision and an inward consciousness. And because it is the adult, formed, and developed consciousness which is degraded into this state of sensitivity, it retains along with its content a certain nominal self-hood, a formal vision and awareness, which, however, does not go so far as the conscious judgement or discernment by which its contents, when it is healthy and awake, exist for it as an outward objectivity. The individual is thus a monad which is inwardly aware of its actuality -- a genius which beholds itself. The characteristic point in such knowledge is that the very same facts (which for the healthy consciousness are an objective practical reality, and to know which, in its sober moods, it needs the intelligent chain of means and conditions in all their real expansion) are now immediately known and perceived in this immanence. This perception is a sort of clairvoyance; for it is a consciousness living in the undivided substantiality of the genius, and finding itself in the very heart of the interconnection, and so can dispense with the series of conditions, external one to another, which lead up to the result -- conditions which cool reflection has in succession to traverse and in so doing feels the limits of its own external individuality. But such clairvoyance -- just because its dim and turbid vision does not present the facts in a rational interconnection -- is for that very reason at the mercy of every private contingency of feeling and fancy, etc. -- not to mention that foreign suggestions (see later) intrude into its vision. It is thus impossible to make out whether what the clairvoyants really see preponderates over what they deceive themselves in.-- But it is absurd to treat this visionary state as a sublime mental phase and as a truer state, capable of conveying general truths.

(d) An essential feature of this sensitivity, with its absence of intelligent and volitional personality, is this, that it is a state of passivity, like that of the child in the womb. The patient in this condition is accordingly made, and continues to be, subject to the power of another person, the magnetizer; so that when the two are thus in psychical rapport, the selfless individual, not really a 'person', has for his subjective consciousness the consciousness of the other. This latter self-possessed individual is thus the effective subjective soul of the former, and the genius which may even supply him with a train of ideas. That the somnambulist perceives in himself tastes and smells which are present in the person with whom he stands en rapport, and that he is aware of the other inner ideas and present perceptions of the latter as if they were his own, shows the substantial identity which the soul (which even in its concreteness is also truly immaterial) is capable of holding with another. When the substance of both is thus made one, there is only one subjectivity of consciousness: the patient has a sort of individuality, but it is empty, not on the spot, not actual: and this nominal self accordingly derives its whole stock of ideas from the sensations and ideas of the other, in whom it sees, smells, tastes, reads, and hears. It is further to be noted on this point that the somnambulist is thus brought into rapport with two genii and a twofold set of ideas, his own and that of the magnetizer. But it is impossible to say precisely which sensations and which visions he, in this nominal perception, receives, beholds, and brings to knowledge from his own inward self, and which from the suggestions of the person with whom he stands in relation. This uncertainty may be the source of many deceptions, and accounts among other things for the diversity that inevitably shows itself among sonmambulists from different countries and under rapport with persons of different education, as regards their views on morbid states and the methods of cure, or medicines for them, as well as on scientific and intellectual topics.

(e) As in this sensitive substantiality there is no contrast to external objectivity, so within itself the subject is so entirely one that all varieties of sensation have disappeared, and hence, when the activity of the sense-organs is asleep, the 'common sense', or 'general feeling' specifies itself to several functions; one sees and hears with the fingers, and especially with the pit of the stomach, etc.

To comprehend a thing means in the language of practical intelligence to be able to trace the series of means intervening between a phenomenon and some other existence on which it depends -- to discover what is called the ordinary course of nature, in compliance with the laws and relations of the intellect, for example, causality, reasons, etc. The purely sensitive life, on the contrary, even when it retains that mere nominal consciousness, as in the morbid state alluded to, is just this form of immediacy, without any distinctions between subjective and objective, between intelligent personality and objective world, and without the aforementioned finite ties between them. Hence to understand this intimate conjunction, which, though all-embracing, is without any definite points of attachment, is impossible, so long as we assume independent personalities, independent one of another and of the objective world which is their content -- so long as we assume the absolute spatial and material externality of one part of being to another.

(b) Self-feeling (sense of self)

i. Particular Feeling

The sensitive totality is, in its capacity as individual, essentially the tendency to distinguish itself in itself, and to wake up to the judgement in itself, in virtue of which it has particular feelings and stands as a subject in respect of these aspects of itself. The subject as such gives these feelings a place as its own in itself. In these private and personal sensations it is immersed, and at the same time, because of the 'ideality' of the particulars, it combines itself in them with itself as a subjective unit. In this way it is self- feeling, and is so at the same time only in the particular feeling.

ii. Insanity

In consequence of the immediacy, which still marks the self-feeling, i.e. in consequence of the element of corporeality which is still undetached from the mental life, and as the feeling too is itself particular and bound up with a special corporeal form, it follows that although the subject has been brought to acquire intelligent consciousness, it is still susceptible of disease, so far as to remain fast in a special phase of its self-feeling, unable to refine it to 'ideality' and get the better of it. The fully furnished self of intelligent consciousness is a conscious subject, which is consistent in itself according to an order and behaviour which follows from its individual position and its connection with the external world, which is no less a world of law. But when it is engrossed with a single phase of feeling, it fails to assign that phase its proper place and due subordination in the individual system of the world which a conscious subject is. In this way the subject finds itself in contradiction between the totality systematized in its consciousness, and the single phase or fixed idea which is not reduced to its proper place and rank. This is Insanity or mental Derangement.

In considering insanity we must, as in other cases, anticipate the full-grown and intelligent conscious subject, which is at the same time the natural self of self-feeling. In such a phase the self can be liable to the contradiction between its own free subjectivity and a particularity which, instead of being 'idealized' in the former, remains as a fixed element in self-feeling. Mind as such is free, and therefore not susceptible of this malady. But in older metaphysics mind was treated as a soul, as a thing; and it is only as a thing, i.e. as something natural and existent, that it is liable to insanity -- the settled fixture of some finite element in it. Insanity is therefore a psychical disease, i.e. a disease of body and mind alike: the commencement may appear to start from the one more than the other, and so also may the cure.

The self-possessed and healthy subject has an active and present consciousness of the ordered whole of his individual world, into the system of which he subsumes each special content of sensation, idea, desire, inclination, etc., as it arises, so as to insert them in their proper place, He is the dominant genius over these particularities. Between this and insanity the difference is like that between waking and dreaming: only that in insanity the dream falls within the waking limits, and so makes part of the actual self- feeling. Error and that sort of thing is a proposition consistently admitted to a place in the objective interconnection of things. In the concrete, however, it is often difficult to say where it begins to become derangement. A violent, but groundless and senseless outburst of hatred, etc., may, in contrast to a presupposed higher self-possession and stability of character, make its victim seem to be beside himself with frenzy. But the main point in derangement is the contradiction which a feeling with a fixed corporeal embodiment sets up against the whole mass of adjustments forming the concrete consciousness. The mind which is in a condition of mere being, and where such being is not rendered fluid in its consciousness, is diseased. The contents which are set free in this reversion to mere nature are the self-seeking affections of the heart, such as vanity, pride, and the rest of the passions -- fancies and hopes -- merely personal love and hatred. When the influence of self-possession and of general principles, moral and theoretical, is relaxed, and ceases to keep the natural temper under lock and key, the, earthly elements are set free -- that evil which is always latent in the heart, because the heart as immediate is natural and selfish. It is the evil genius of man which gains the upper hand in insanity, but in distinction from and contrast to the better and more intelligent part, which is there also. Hence this state is mental derangement and distress. The right psychical treatment therefore keeps in view the truth that insanity is not an abstract loss of reason (neither in the point of intelligence nor of will and its responsibility), but only derangement, only a contradiction in a still subsisting reason; -- just as physical disease is not an abstract, i.e. mere and total, loss of health (if it were that, it would be death), but a contradiction in it. This humane treatment, no less benevolent than reasonable (the services of Pinel towards which deserve the highest acknowledgement), presupposes the patient's rationality, and in that assumption has the sound basis for dealing with him on this side -- just as in the case of bodily disease the physician bases his treatment on the vitality which as such still contains health.

(c) Habit

Self-feeling, immersed in the detail of the feelings (in simple sensations, and also desires, instincts, passions, and their gratification), is undistinguished from them. But in the self there is latent a simple self-relation of ideality, a nominal universality (which is the truth of these details): and as so universal, the self is to be stamped upon, and made appear in, this life of feeling, yet so as to distinguish itself from the particular details, and be a realized universality. But this universality is not the full and sterling truth of the specific feelings and desires; what they specifically contain is as yet left out of account. And so too the particularity is, as now regarded, equally formal; it counts only as the particular being or immediacy of the soul in opposition to its equally formal and abstract realization. This particular being of the soul is the factor of its corporeity; here we have it breaking with this corporeity, distinguishing it from itself -- itself a simple being -- and becoming the 'ideal', subjective substantiality of it -- just as in its latent notion it was the substance, and the mere substance, of it.

But this abstract realization of the soul in its corporeal vehicle is not yet the self -- not the existence of the universal which is for the universal. It is the corporeity reduced to its mere ideality; and so far only does corporeity belong to the soul as such. That is to say, just as space and time as the abstract one-outside-another, as, therefore, empty space and empty time, are only subjective forms, a pure act of intuition; so is that pure being (which, through the supersession in it of the particularity of the corporeity, or of the immediate corporeity as such, has realized itself) mere intuition and no more, lacking consciousness, but the basis of consciousness. And consciousness it becomes, when the corporcity, of which it is the subjective substance, and which still continues to exist, and that as a barrier for it, has been absorbed by it, and it has been invested with the character of self-centred subject.

The soul's making itself an abstract universal being, and reducing the particulars of feelings (and of consciousness) to a mere feature of its being is Habit. In this manner the soul has the contents in possession, and contains them in such manner that in these features it is not as sentient, nor does it stand in relationship with them as distinguishing itself from them, nor is absorbed in them, but has them and moves in them, without feeling or consciousness of the fact. The soul is freed from them, so far as it is not interested in or occupied with them: and whilst existing in these forms as its possession, it is at the same time open to be otherwise occupied and engaged -- say with feeling and with mental consciousness in general.

This process of building up the particular and corporeal expressions of feeling into the being of the soul appears as a repetition of them, and the generation of habit as practice. For, this being of the soul, if in respect of the natural particular phase it be called an abstract universality to which the former is transmuted, is a reflexive universality ; i.e. the one and the same, that recurs in a series of units of sensation, is reduced to unity, and this abstract unity expressly stated.

Habit like memory, is a difficult point in mental organization: habit is the mechanism of self-feeling, as memory is the mechanism of intelligence. The natural qualities and alterations of age, sleep, and waking are 'immediately' natural: habit, on the contrary, is the mode of feeling (as well as intelligence, will, etc., so far as they belong to self-feeling) made into a natural and mechanical existence. Habit is rightly called a second nature; nature, because it is an immediate being of the soul; a second nature, because it is an immediacy created by the soul, impressing and moulding the corporeality which enters into the modes of feeling as such and into the representations and volitions so far as they have taken corporeal form .

In habit the human being's mode of existence is 'natural', and for that reason not free; but still free, so far as the merely natural phase of feeling is by habit reduced to a mere being of his, and he is no longer involuntarily attracted or repelled by it, and so no longer interested, occupied, or dependent in regard to it. The want of freedom in habit is partly merely formal, as habit merely attaches to the being of the soul; partly only relative, so far as it strictly speaking arises only in the case of bad habits, or so far as a habit is opposed by another purpose: whereas the habit of right and goodness is an embodiment of liberty. The main point about Habit is that by its means man gets emancipated from the feelings, even in being affected by them. The different forms of this may be described as follows:

(a) The immediate feeling is negated and treated as indifferent. One who gets inured against external sensations (frost, heat, weariness of the limbs, etc., sweet tastes, etc.), and who hardens the heart against misfortune, acquires a strength which consists in this, that although the frost, etc. -- or the misfortune -- is felt, the affection is deposed to a mere externality and immediacy; the universal psychical life keeps its own abstract independence in it, and the self-feeling as such, consciousness, reflection, and any other purposes and activity, are no longer bothered with it.

(b) There is indifference towards the satisfaction: the desires and impulses are by the habit of their satisfaction deadened. This is the rational liberation from them; whereas monastic renunciation and forcible interference do not free from them, nor are they in conception rational. Of course in all this it is assumed that the impulses are kept as the finite modes they naturally are, and that they, like their satisfaction, are subordinated as partial factors to the reasonable will.

(c) In habit regarded as aptitude, or skill, not merely has the abstract psychical life to be kept intact per se, but it has to be imposed as a subjective aim, to be made a power in the bodily part, which is rendered subject and thoroughly pervious to it. Conceived as having the inward purpose of the subjective soul thus imposed upon it, the body is treated as an immediate externality and a barrier. Thus comes out the more decided rupture between the soul as simple self- concentration, and its earlier naturalness and immediacy; it has lost its original and immediate identity with the bodily nature, and as external has first to be reduced to that position. Specific feelings can only get bodily shape in a perfectly specific way; and the immediate portion of body is a particular possibility for a specific aim (a particular aspect of its differentiated structure, a particular organ of its organic system). To mould such an aim in the organic body is to bring out and express the 'ideality' which is implicit in matter always, and especially so in the specific bodily part, and thus to enable the soul, under its volitional and conceptual characters, to exist as substance in its corporeity. In this way an aptitude shows the corporeity rendered completely pervious, made into an instrument, so that when the conception (e.g. a series of musical notes) is in me, then without resistance and with ease the body gives them correct utterance.

The form of habit applies to all kinds and grades of mental action. The most external of them, i.e. the spatial direction of an individual, viz. his upright posture, has been by will made a habit -- a position taken without adjustment and without consciousness -- which continues to be an affair of his persistent will; for the man stands only because and in so far as he wills to stand, and only so long as he wills it without consciousness. Similarly our eyesight is the concrete habit which, without an express adjustment, combines in a single act the several modifications of sensation, consciousness, intuition, intelligence, etc., which make it up. Thinking, too, however free and active in its own pure element it becomes, no less requires habit and familiarity (this impromptuity or form of immediacy), by which it is the property of my single self where I can freely and in all directions range. It is through this habit that I come to realize my existence as a thinking being. Even here, in this spontaneity of self-centred thought, there is a partnership of soul and body (hence, want of habit and too-long-continued thinking cause headache); habit diminishes this feeling, by making the natural function an immediacy of the soul. Habit on an ampler scale, and carried out in the strictly intellectual range, is recollection and memory, whereof we shall speak later.

Habit is often spoken of disparagingly and called lifeless, casual, and particular. And it is true that the form of habit, like any other, is open to anything we chance to put into it; and it is habit of living which brings on death, or, if quite abstract, is death itself: and yet habit is indispensable for the existence of all intellectual life in the individual, enabling the subject to be a concrete immediacy, an 'ideality' of soul -- enabling the matter of consciousness, religious, moral, etc., to be his as this self, this soul, and no other, and be neither a mere latent possibility, nor a transient emotion or idea, nor an abstract inwardness, cut off from action and reality, but part and parcel of his being. In scientific studies of the soul and the mind, habit is usually passed over -- either as something contemptible -- or rather for the further reason that it is one of the most difficult questions of psychology.

(c) THE ACTUAL SOUL

The Soul, when its corporeity has been moulded and made thoroughly its own, finds itself there a single subject; and the corporeity is an externality which stands as a predicate, in being related to which, it is related to itself. This externality, in other words, represents not itself, but the soul, of which it is the sign. In this identity of interior and exterior, the latter subject to the former, the soul is actual: in its corporeity it has its free shape, in which it feels itself and makes itself felt, and which as the Soul's work of art has human pathognomic and physiognomic expression.

Under the head of human expression are included, for example, the upright figure in general, and the formation of the limbs, especially the hand, as the absolute instrument, of the mouth -- laughter, weeping, etc., and the note of mentality diffused over the whole, which at once announces the body as the externality of a higher nature. This note is so slight, indefinite, and inexpressible a modification, because the figure in its externality is something immediate and natural, and can therefore only be an indefinite and quite imperfect sign for the mind, unable to represent it in its actual universality. Seen from the animal world, the human figure is the supreme phase in which mind makes an appearance. But for the mind it is only its first appearance, while language is its perfect expression. And the human figure, though the proximate phase of mind's existence, is at the same time in its physiognomic and pathognomic quality something contingent to it. To try to raise physiognomy and above all cranioscopy (phrenology) to the rank of sciences, was therefore one of the vainest fancies, still vainer than a signatura rerum, which supposed the shape of a plant to afford indication of its medicinal virtue.

Implicitly the soul shows the untruth and unreality of matter; for the soul, in its concentrated self, cuts itself off from its immediate being, placing the latter over against it as a corporeity incapable of offering resistance to its moulding influence. The soul, thus setting in opposition its being to its (conscious) self, absorbing it, and making it its own, has lost the meaning of mere soul, or the 'immediacy' of mind. The actual soul with its sensation and its concrete self-feeling turned into habit, has implicitly realised the 'ideality' of its qualities; in this externality it has recollected and inwardized itself, and is infinite self-relation. This free universality thus made explicit shows the soul awaking to the higher stage of the ego, or abstract universality, in so far as it is for the abstract universality. In this way it gains the position of thinker and subject -- specially a subject of the judgement in which the ego excludes from itself the sum total of its merely natural features as an object, a world external to it -- but with such respect to that object that in it it is immediately reflected into itself. Thus soul rises to become Consciousness.

A. The Soul

(a) Natural Determinacy
(b) Antithesis to Substance
(c) Reality of Soul

Spirit came into being as the truth of nature which has translated and suspended itself But spirit is, then, not merely true and primordial: its transition into the realm of the concept is not only reflection into others and reflection into itself but it is also free judgment. The becoming of spirit in this way indicates that nature suspends itself in itself as untruth, and that spirit no longer presupposes itself as immediacy self-externalised in physical individuality, but as general and as that immediacy, simple in its concreteness, in which it is soul.

The soul is not only immaterial for itself but the general immateriality of nature and its simple, ideal life. The soul is also the absolute substance, as the immediate identity of self-subsisting subjectivity and corporeality, whose identity remains, as general essence, the absolute basis of its differentiation and individuation. In this abstract determination, however, it is only the sleep of the spirit.

The question of the immateriality of the soul can only be of interest if matter is represented as true, on the one hand, and on the other hand, if spirit is represented as a thing. Even physicists, however, have in recent times dealt with imponderable substances, such as warmth, light, and so on, to which they could also add space and time. Otherwise these imponderables still have a sensory existence, a self-externalised being. Yet living matter, which can be found included among such substances, lacks not only gravity, but every other aspect of existence which would allow us to treat it as material. The fact is that in the idea of life the self-externality of nature is already in itself suspended, along with the concept and its substance. But in the spirit, the concept exists in freedom as absolute negativity and not as immediate individuality, so that the object of the intelligible unity is the unity itself Thus self-externality, as the fundamental characteristic of matter, is completely dissolved and transformed into generality.

Another related question concerns the interdependence of the soul and the body. It was assumed as a fact, and the only remaining problem was how to comprehend it. The usual answer was that it was an incomprehensible secret. And indeed, if we take them to be absolutely antithetical and absolutely independent, body and soul are just as impenetrable to each other as every part of matter is to another. In this view they respond to each other only in the pores, their reciprocal being where the other is not. But this answer is not the same as the one given by all other philosophers since the relation was first questioned. Descartes, Malebranche, Spinoza, and Leibniz have all seen God as this relation, especially in the sense that the finite soul and matter have no truth, so that God is not merely another word for that incomprehensibility, but rather its true identity. Either this identity, however, is not yet grasped immediately as God, for it does not yet have this determination, or the soul itself is seen as a general soul, in which matter exists in its truth, as a simple thought or a generality.-- This soul must not, however, become fixed again, for example as the world soul, for then it is only the general substance which merely has actual truth as individuality.

Spirit is at first this immediate submergence in nature: (a) the soul in its determination as nature; (b) as the soul is particularised, it emerges in antithesis to its lack of consciousness; (c) in the process it acquires corporeality, and thus becomes real.

(a) The Natural Determinacy of the Soul

Spirit as the abstract soul of nature is simple, sidereal, and terrestrial life. It is the nous of the ancients, the simple, unconscious thought, which (a) as this general essence is the inner idea and would have its reality in the underlying externality of nature. But since it, as soul, is immediate substance, its existence is the particularisation of its natural being, an immediate and natural determinacy, which has its presupposed reality in the individual earth.

The general planetary life of the nature spirit has the diversity of the earth as immediate differentiation within it; it then dissolves into particular spirits of nature, which wholly express the nature of the geographic parts of the world and constitute racial diversity.

The contrast between the earth's poles, by which the northern land is more compressed and more heavily weighted than the sea, whereas the southern hemisphere separates and disperses into widely distant peaks, introduces into the differences between continents a further modification which Treviranus (Biology, part 2) has exhibited in the case of the plants and animals.

This diversity is transformed by the contingency of nature into particularities, which may be called local spirits, and manifests itself in outward forms of life and occupation, physical development and disposition, but even more in the inner tendency and capacity of intellectual and moral character.

The soul, as the concept in itself in general, isolates itself as the individual subject. But this subjectivity is here considered only as the individuation of natural characteristics; it is the mode of the different temperaments, characters, physiognomies, and other dispositions of families or single individuals.

(b) Immediate judgment is the awakening of the individual soul, which confronts its unconscious natural life, in the first instance as one natural characteristic and condition confronts another, namely, sleep. This transitional phase of individuality connects with the earth as the general body of individuality.

Waking is neither externally nor for us intrinsically different from sleep; rather, waking is itself the judgment of the individual soul, and thus the differentiation of itself from its undifferentiated generality. All self-conscious and rational activity of the spirit occurs in the waking state.-- Sleep is an invigoration of this activity, though not in the sense of rest (the power of living action actually becomes sluggish due to the lack of its expression), but as a return from the world of specialisation, from dispersion into details where it has become rigidified, into the general essence of subjectivity, which is the substance of those specialised energies and their absolute master.

Insofar, however, as the entire being of the individual is an awakened being, its particularisation is the natural development of an age.

(c) Real individuality as the reflection of the soul in itself is its waking being for itself in self-contained, organic physicality. It also involves a self-feeling determined in and for itself and still identical with its corporeality, external and internal sensation.

The progress of the general soul to an individuality which is still immediate is above all the progress of the natural idea, from ideal generality to -vitality, that is, organic individualism In any case this has no further meaning than that it contains the spirit in itself and this is its individual and natural existence, which, however, exists here only in external representation. As in the previous case, therefore, what can be said more precisely about wakefulness as a specific waking of the spirit, and about the course of an age in the unique meaning of its intellectual development, must be seen as anticipated or as taken from representation.-- On the natural side of this immanence of the individual spirit in its physicality falls in general the healthy and sympathetic sense of community. Belonging here, then, are not only the external feelings of the senses considered above, but also the sensations, determined more precisely as immediately symbolic, including colours, smells, sounds, either immediately attractive or repulsive, either in a more general or in a more idiosyncratic manner. Under this rubric would also be found not only the inner sympathy of the parts of the body, but also certain mental qualities, such as the passions or the emotions. It is important to include here the line of connection by which anger and courage are felt in the breast, the blood, desire in the reproductive system, irritation, and contemplation, intellectual activity in the head, which is also considered the centre of the sensible system.

(b) The Antithesis of the Subjective Soul to Its Substance

The soul, which lives at first immediately in its substantial identity, is in its individuality as a negative self-relation, and the division of its subjectivity is set against its substantial life, which is incompatible with its concept. This first reflection into itself is at the same time a reflection into another; it stands at first, therefore, only in relation to its natural determination.

The subject is (a) in an abstract and general relation to its natural life; the soul is, to be sure, the subject from this perspective, but its predicate in this general relation is still its substance, an impotent, merely formal being for itself a sense of foreboding and dreaming of its more general natural life, the feeling of the nature spirit.

This relation rests on the dividing line of the spirit from itself as soul. Spirit as such has generality for its object as a thought entity, pure, that is, with its abstract subjectivity, identical with its selfhood, and its relationship to it is itself this thought. This certain substantiality is freedom, the pure negativity of all immediacy. Such free substantiality is already a part of pure self-consciousness and the actual spirit.

Thus the present, unfree matter is a reduction of free self-consciousness, -- a disease in which the soul, which according to Plato delivers prophecies in the liver, or more definitely in the ganglia than in the brain or the belly. Spirit in this instance has sunken back into the spirit of nature.-- In history this magical relation, which can occur in isolated individuals as a diseased condition, constitutes a phase of transition from substantial spirituality to self-consciousness and understanding.-- Forebodings, prophecies, the many miraculous aspects of dreams, and other tendencies, somnambulism and animal magnetism: all these belong more or less to the realm of dream in general, where the spirit hovers between natural spirits and its rational reality, and produces thereby a representation of its more general connection in a larger natural sphere than the sort of consciousness which has understood and reasoned about itself But since real generality, namely that of thought, only adheres to this consciousness, then that expansion of sympathetic life which emerges as representation is limited absolutely to a particular circle, and what this soul sees and predicts is only its particular inferiority, not that of a general essence. But this magical circle is ultimately an incantation, a form of subjugation, a dependency, because the soul is reduced from its free generality to particularity. Thus the image of humanity's primitive condition, in which nature and the spirit do not appear externally to inner intuition but with pure immediacy, becomes diminished daily, as with few aspects of the tradition, and dwindles into an ever-weaker position. It becomes an empty assumption, by which the general nature of the idea as a reasonable thought, which belongs only to the spirit in its free subjectivity, remains unobserved.

(b) The subjective soul itself however, breaks the immediate, substantial identity of its relation with particular, natural being. Its antithesis, which is at the same time an identity, is a relation of contradiction: a condition of disruption, in which both aspects of the relation emerge in reality against each other and corporeal reality becomes the reality of the soul, or conversely, the soul constructs its own reality as corporeal.

This relation is the condition of madness in general. It should at the same time be remarked that: (I) this relation, like the magical relation, exists merely as ideal moments, as untrue relations, and thus persists only as conditions or diseases of the spirit. Precisely as everything finite persists, and, more specifically, just as the formal judgment and the formal syllogism exist without truth and apply only to the abstract moments of the objective concept, thus it has only a violent existence and is grounded in destruction, -- a destruction which the understanding causes as it transforms the concrete into abstractions solely through its reality. Thus the relations which have now emerged are only the ideal moments of the spirit free in being, and still dominated by the hypothetic judgment. They are still substantially related to their substance in their self-differentiating subjectivity, and just as essentially the contradiction in this relation, their being is above all not their being, but exists rather as the being of their other.

(2) On this level of the relation the spirit is determined as a thing, and more precisely, as that which is understood as soul. To the ancients, for whom the antithesis of thought and being had not yet been as fully actualised, the soul had the more indeterminate meaning of spirituality. By contrast, in more recent metaphysics and other representations the spirit as soul has become a thing of many characteristics and powers, fixed as a spectre, or more precisely as an angel, and even decorated with a colour as a sensory entity. Metaphysics has generally held to the abstract determination of a thing, and the soul therefore has

in and for itself the determinations of being, of quality and quantity, and is subordinated to the reflective categories of individual substances, causes, and so on. Here the question of the location of the soul, of the connection between this thing and the other thing, the body, has been of interest.

It is a contribution of Kant's to have weighed the metaphysics of spirit and soul as things and, what is the same, to have freed the spirit from this metaphysics and representation and to have posited the self in its place. For the spirit as thing can only be spoken of in a relation, that is, on the level of reflection, where the spirit of course loses its immediate substantiality or its subsisting universality, and determines itself as difference and as subject, although it has not yet achieved true reality.

(3) The different forms of madness, -- insanity, wildness, raving, nonsense, are shadings which contain many indeterminate qualities, concerning the determinations which they have in contrast to each other, just as they themselves confront conditions which common sense accepts. As important as this differentiation is for the treatment of these diseases, it is at the same time a perversion to want to create an awareness of human beings on that basis, as well as on the basis of crimes and other depravities and disturbances of humanity. To recognise these disorders presupposes in fact a concept of what the human being should be.

Moreover, in all forms of disease it is not only possible to observe a lack of understanding, but also to see what is actually called madness. For it is the absolute unhappiness of contradiction that the spirit, which is the free identity of subjective and objective, exists in its serfhood not as absolute ideality, but as an actual thing, and exists just as much as an objective entity in contrast to the thing as its pure identity. As such it is the relation of necessity or of finite reciprocal effect, of immediate transformation and reversal. This madness, in other words, grasps fate purely as blind fate, that is as absolute alienation from the concept, and as such it is after all identical with itself knowing itself at once to be and not to be itself- Distraction can be seen as the beginning of madness; in it is the spirit in itself and it has no present in its corporeality, though it does exist in it, and mistakenly reverses the situation. The highest level is anger, whereby the singularity of serfhood fixes arbitrariness in its pure abstraction against the objective idea into a static reality, and exchanges itself with pure will.

Psychic treatment rests on the insight that madness is not the loss of reason, from the side of both the intellect and the will, but is only madness, and presupposes therefore the treatment of the sick as reasonable beings, thereby providing a fixed basic assumption on which the rest can build.

(c) The soul is substantial, however, as the general concept for itself the overarching power and fate of the other reality which is essentially its own immediacy. The soul's relation to judgment is, therefore, a suspension of its form and the positing of the form as its own.

Because it is originally identical to this corporeality, and has its reality in it, the soul's activity is not directed against the body as against an external and antagonistic object. To injure organic life and to foster an antagonistic, destructive treatment of corporeality would instead make this into a negative objectivity aimed against the subject, producing thereby a power and a fate, and would derange the standpoint of the spirit.

The activity of the soul against the body is, rather, to establish its self-subsisting identity with its corporeality, only to suspend the form of the immediacy of this unity, and to posit as general the pervasive soul in its body for itself.

The soul forms itself then, in the body which it has from nature. It builds up, in this immediate being, its generality through the repetition of actions purposively determined, through induction. Thus it remembers itself in the body in such a way, on the one hand, that its identity with the body is determined by the soul and forms its subjective unity with itself On the other hand, it achieves being in the body, a being as a general habit, a determinate habit, and as historical authenticity. In this way, as a thoroughly formed instrument, it dominates the body.

(c) The Reality of the Soul

The soul, in its thoroughly formed corporeality, exists as an individual subject, and the corporeality is an externality which stands as a predicate of the subject, which in this way only relates to itself in itself This externality thus does not represent itself but the soul, of which it is the sign. In this identity of interior and exterior the soul is actual, and has only in its corporeality its free shape, its human, pathognomonic and physiognomic expression.

Under the heading of human expression are included, for example, the upright figure in general, the formation of limbs, especially the hand, as the absolute instrument, of the mouth, of laughter, weeping, and so on, and the intellectual tone diffused over the whole, which immediately announces the body as the exteriority of a higher nature. This tone is a slight, indefinite, an inexpressible modification. For the spirit is identical with its general exteriority and thus free, whereas the shape is immediate and natural, and can therefore only be an indefinite sign for the spirit, for it represents the spirit as an other, and not for itself in its generality. For the animal, then, the human figure is the highest form in which the spirit appears. But for the spirit it is only its first appearance, because it is reality still sunken in the sphere of immediacy.-- Spirit is, therefore, absolutely finite and isolated in the human figure as sign. It is, to be sure, its existent form, but at the same time the human figure is something entirely contingent in its physiognomic and pathognomonic determinacy for the spirit. Thus to want to raise physiognomy and, above all, cranioscopy (phrenology) to the level of sciences is one of the emptiest ideas there could be, emptier than a signature rerum, which supposed that the shape of a plant would reveal its true medicinal uses.

In and for itself spirit as the general soul shows the untruth of matter. Corporeality, which is at first nothing but a form of immediacy, can therefore achieve its formation in general and without any resistance. Through this first formation of being in itself the spirit, which will be against it, is suspended, has lost its own determinate meaning of the soul, and becomes an "I".

This infinity of the spirit as the relationship of itself to itself in its immediacy is its own suspension, which has been produced first and is therefore still a moment, though against and in this infinity. What is included here with itself in otherness is also determinate individuality, which is the subject for itself and contains itself as this negativity. The judgment, in which the subject becomes "I" in contrast to an object, as if in contrast to a foreign world, is thus reflected immediately into itself Thus the soul becomes consciousness.

B. Consciousness

(a) Consciousness as Such
(b) Self-Consciousness
(c) Reason

Consciousness constitutes the reflected or relational level of the spirit, the level of its appearance. The self is the infinite relation of the spirit to itself but a subjective relation, as self-certainty. As this absolute negativity it is identity in its otherness; the self is itself and extends over the object, it is one side of the relation and the whole relation; -- the light, which manifests both itself and the other.

But the identity is only formal. The spirit as soul is in the form of substantial generality; as self-subsisting gravity, it is related as subjective reflection in itself to darkness. And consciousness is, like relationship in general, the contradiction between the independence of the two sides and their identity in which they are suspended.

The object, as it is released by the infinite reflection of the spirit in its judgment, has this finite relation to itself as its essence, and is a subsisting and a given entity in contrast to the being for itself of the self.

Since the self does not exist as the concept, but only as a formal identity, the dialectical movement of consciousness does not seem to it to be its own activity, but seems to occur in itself that is, as a change in the object. Consciousness appears differently, therefore, according to the differences in the given object, and the ongoing development of consciousness appears as a development of the object. The observation of its necessary changes, however, the concept, falls, because it is still as such interior, within us.

Kantian philosophy may be most accurately described as having conceived of the spirit as consciousness, and as containing only determinations of the phenomenology, not the philosophy, of spirit. Kant views the self as the relation to a "thing in itself" lying somewhere beyond, and it is only from this perspective that he treats the intellect and the will. Though with the concept of reflecting judgment he does speak of the idea of the spirit, subject-objectivity, an intuitive understanding, and so on, and even the idea of nature, this idea is itself demoted to an appearance again, namely, to a subjective principle. Reinhold, it may therefore be said, correctly understood Kantianism, when he treated it as a theory of consciousness, under the name of the faculty of imagination. Fichtean philosophy adheres to the same point of view, for his "not-I" is only an object of the "I," only determined as in consciousness; it remains an infinite impulse, that is, a thing in itself Both philosophies show, therefore, that they have not clearly reached the concept or the spirit as it is in and for itself but only as it is in relation to something else.

The aim of the spirit as consciousness is to make its appearance identical with its essence, to raise the certainty of itself to truth. The existence of the spirit in consciousness is formal or general as such; because that is determined only abstractly, or it is only self-reflected as an abstract self its existence retains a content which is not yet its own.

The levels of this elevation of certainty to truth are: (a) consciousness in general, which has an object as such; (b) self-consciousness, for which the self is the object; (c) the unity of consciousness and self-consciousness, where the spirit sees itself as the content of the object and as in and for itself determinate; -- as reason, the concept of the spirit.

(a) Consciousness as Such

Consciousness is: (I) immediate consciousness, and its relation to the object is accordingly the simple, unmediated certainty of it. The object itself is subsisting, but as it is reflected in itself it is determined further as immediately individual. This is sensory consciousness.

To sensory consciousness belongs the categories of feeling as content, external or internal, and spatial and temporal experience as form. But these both belong to the spirit in its concrete form, both as feelings and as intuitions. Consciousness as a case of relation comprises only the categories belonging to the abstract self and these it treats as features of the object.

Sensory consciousness therefore apprehends the object immediately as subsisting, a something, an existing thing, an individual entity, and its immediacy as determined in and for itself What the object is otherwise in its concrete form concerns the spirit; the self as a concrete entity is the spirit. Even the categories of feeling are only sensory in the form of immediacy; their contents can be of a quite other nature. In consciousness, the self is still abstract thought and has initially as object, therefore, the abstract categories of thought. Spatial and temporal singularity is the here and the now, and the object of sensory consciousness, as I determined in my Phenomenology of Spirit (Werke 2 p. 73). More essentially, the object is to be taken only according to the identity of the relation by which it has its determination. In this way it exists for consciousness only as an external entity, neither externally for itself nor a being external to itself The other can achieve this freedom only through the freedom of the spirit.

The sensory as something becomes an other; the reflection of something in itself the thing, has many qualities, and as a single individual it exists in its immediacy as manifold predicates. The many individual moments of sensory consciousness become therefore a broad field, a multiplicity of relations, categories of reflection, and generalities. As the object is so changed, sensory consciousness becomes sense perception.

(2) Consciousness, having passed beyond the sensory level, wants to grasp the object in its truth, not as merely immediate, but as mediated, reflected in itself and general. Such an object is a combination of sensory qualities and categories of thought; consciousness here combines concrete relations and reflection into itself In this way its identity with the object is no longer the abstract one of certainty, but now the determinate identity of knowledge.

The particular level of consciousness at which Kantian philosophy conceives the spirit is perception, which is in general the standpoint of our ordinary consciousness, and more or less of the sciences. The sensory certainties of individual apperceptions or observation form the starting point. These are in turn supposed to be elevated to truth by being observed in their relations, reflected upon, and according to categories of the understanding turned at the same time into something necessary and general, into experiences.

This linkage of the individual and the general is a mixture, because the individual remains basically hardened being, whereas the general by contrast is reflected in itself It is, therefore, a many sided contradiction -- between the individual things of sense apperception, which supposedly constitute the ground of general experience, and the general, which supposedly has a higher claim to be the essence and the ground -- between the individuality of things themselves, which constitutes their independence, and their manifold qualities, which are free from this negative bind and from one another, and are independent, general materials.

The truth of perception is the contradiction, instead of the identity of the individual object and the generality of consciousness, or the individuality of the object itself and its generality. The truth is thus that the object is appearance, and that its reflection into itself is an interior subsisting for itself The consciousness which receives this object, into which the object of perception has been transferred, is the understanding.

(3) For the understanding the things of perception count as appearances; their interior, which the understanding has as an object, is, on the one hand, their suspended multiplicity, and in this way it is the abstract identity, but, on the other hand, it also contains the multiplicity, but as internal, simple difference, which remains self-identical in the changes of appearance. This

simple difference is, in the first place, the realm of the laws of phenomena, a copy, but brought to rest and general.

The law, at first as the relation of general, lasting determinations, has, insofar as its difference is the inward one, its necessity in itself; the one of the determinations, as not externally different from the other, lies immediately in the other. But in this way the interior difference is what it is in truth, namely, the difference in itself or the difference which is none.

Consciousness, which as understanding has at first only an abstract interior, then takes the law as its object, and has now found the concept. But insofar as consciousness and the object are still a given, it observes the object as a living entity, -- an inferiority, which is in and for itself determinate generality, or truth.

Self-consciousness is sparked, however, by the consciousness of life; for as consciousness has an object, as an entity different from itself it is also true in life that the difference is no difference. For the immediacy in which the living entity is the object of consciousness is precisely the appearance, or the mode reduced to negation which now, as inner difference, or concept, is the negation of itself against consciousness.

(b) Self-consciousness

The truth of consciousness is self-consciousness, and the latter is the ground of the former, all consciousness of another object being as a matter of fact also self-consciousness. The expression of this is I=I.

In this form, however, it is still without reality: as it is its own object, there is strictly speaking no object as such, for it contains no distinction between it and the object. The self however, the concept for itself is the absolute diremption of judgment. In this way self-consciousness is for itself the drive to suspend and to realise itself.

Since abstract self-consciousness is itself immediate, and the first negation of self-consciousness, it is subsisting and sensually concrete in itself Self-determination is, therefore, on the one hand negation as a moment posited by itself in itself whereas on the other hand it is an external object. Or the whole, which is its object, is the preceding level, consciousness, and it remains this itself.

The drive of self-consciousness is thus to suspend its subjectivity in general; more precisely, to give to abstract knowledge content and objectivity from itself and conversely, to free itself from its sensuality, to suspend objectivity as a given, and to posit itself as identical with itself or to equate its consciousness with its self-consciousness. -- Both are one and the same.

(I) Self-consciousness in its immediacy is a singularity and a desire: the contradiction, implied in its abstraction, which should be objective, or in its immediacy, which should be subjective. As against I = I, the concept is in itself the idea, the unity of itself and its reality.-- Its immediacy, which is determined to be suspended, has at the same time the shape of an external object, which determines that self-consciousness is consciousness. But, for the self-certainty arising from the suspension of consciousness, the object is determined as null in itself Self-consciousness, therefore, is in itself in the object, and in this way conforms with the drive. In the negation, as the proper activity of the self it becomes this identity for the self.

To this activity the object, which implicitly and for self-consciousness is selfless, can offer no resistance: the dialectic, which is, its nature, is to be suspended, and is here an activity which the self perceives at the same time as external. The given object thereby becomes just as subjective as the subjectivity which externalises itself and becomes objective to itself.

The product of the process is that the self in this reality joins itself with itself; but this return yields at first only existence as an individual, because it relates itself only negatively to the selfless object and the object is thereby merely consumed. Thus desire is in its satisfaction always destructive and selfish.

But self-consciousness has in itself already the certainty of itself in the immediate object, the feeling of self which it acquires in the satisfaction and which thus is not abstract being for itself or merely its individuality, but is an objective entity. For the satisfaction is the negation of its own immediacy, and the diremption of this immediacy thus occurs in the consciousness of a free object, in which the self knows of itself as a self.

(2) It is a self-consciousness for a self-consciousness, at first immediately, as an other for an other. I immediately perceive myself in the other as "I," and yet also an immediately existing object, another "I" absolutely independent of me. This contradiction, that I am only I as the negativity of immediate existence, yields the process of recognition.

The process is a struggle. For I can not know of myself in the other as myself insofar as the other is an immediate other existence for me. I consequently concentrate on the suspension of this immediacy. But this immediacy is at the same time the existence of self-consciousness, in which as in its sign and instrument self-consciousness has its own feeling of self and its being for others, and has the general means of entering into relation with them. In the same way I can not be recognised as immediate, except insofar as the "I" suspends the immediacy in myself and thereby brings my freedom into existence.

The struggle for recognition is thus a matter of life and death: either self-consciousness imperils the life of the other and brings itself into danger -- but only into danger, for each is no less determined to preserve its life as the essential moment. Thus the death of one, which from one perspective solves the contradiction -- though by the abstract, therefore crude negation of immediacy -- is yet, from the essential perspective or the existence of recognition, the greater contradiction.

Since life is as essential as freedom is, the struggle ends in the first place -- for in this sphere the immediate individuality of the two self-consciousnesses is presupposed -- as in inequality: whereas one of the fighters prefers life and retains its abstract or individual self-consciousness, but surrenders its claim for recognition, the other holds fast to this universality, and is recognised by the former as inferior. Thus arises the relation of master and servant.

The struggle for recognition and the subjugation under a master are the phenomena in which the social life of people emerges. Force, which is the basis of this phenomenon, is thus not a basis of law, but only the necessary and legitimate moment in the transition from the state of self-consciousness mired in appetite and selfish isolation into the suspension of immediate self-hood. This other, however, overcomes the desire and individuality of sunken self-consciousness and transforms it into the condition of general self-consciousness.

This relation is in the first place and according to its identity a shared feature of the need, the desire, and the concern for satisfaction. In place of the crude destruction of the immediate object there follows the acquisition, preservation, and formation of it, as of the intermediary by which the two extremes of dependence and independence are welded together.

According to the distinction between the two, the master has in the servant and its servitude the intuition of the objectivity of his individual being for itself in its suspension, but only insofar as it belongs to an other. -- The servant, however, in the service of the master, works off his individual or self-will, suspends his inner immediacy, and through this externalisation learns fear of the master and beginning of wisdom, -- the transition to general self-consciousness.

(3) General self-consciousness is the positive knowledge of self in another self: each self as a free individuality has absolute independence, though in virtue of the negation of its immediacy without distinguishing itself from that other. Each is thus general self-consciousness and objective; each has real generality in such a way as it recognises itself in the free other, and knows this insofar as it recognises the other and knows it to be free.

This general reappearance of self-consciousness, the concept, which knows itself in its objectivity as a subjectivity identical with itself and therefore general, is the substance of all true spiritual life, of the family, the fatherland, the state, and of all virtues, -- love, friendship, bravery, honour, fame.

This unity of consciousness and self-consciousness has in the first place individuals existing in contrast to each other as beings for themselves. But their difference in this identity is entirely indeterminate diversity, or rather it is a difference which is none. Hence its truth is the unmediated generality subsisting in and for itself and the objectivity of self-consciousness, -- reason.

(c) Reason

The essential and real truth which reason is, exists in the simple identity of the subjectivity of the concept with its objectivity and generality. The generality of reason has, therefore, the meaning of the object given in consciousness as well as the self in consciousness.

Reason has, therefore, as the pure individuality of the certainty that the categories of self-consciousness are just as objective, categories of the essence of things as its own thoughts.

As this identity reason is the absolute substance, which is truth. The unique determinacy which it has here, after the object presupposed against the self has suspended its one-sidedness as much as the self set against the object, -- is the substantial truth, whose determinacy is the concept itself subsisting purely for itself, I, -- the certainty of itself as an infinite generality. This knowing truth is the spirit.Encyclopaedia of the Philosophical Sciences

C. Spirit

(a) Theoretical Spirit
(b) Practical Spirit

Spirit has shown itself as the unity of the soul and consciousness, -- the former a simple immediate totality, and the latter is knowledge which is not limited by any object, and no longer stands in relation to it, but is knowledge of the simple, neither subjective nor objective totality. Spirit originates, therefore, only from its own being, and only relates itself to its own determinations.

The soul is finite, insofar as it is immediate or determined by nature; consciousness is finite, insofar as it has an object; and spirit is finite, insofar as it immediately has determinacy in itself or insofar as the determinacy is posited by spirit. In and for itself it is absolutely infinite objective reason, which is defined as its concept and its reality, knowledge, or intelligence. Hence the finitude of spirit consists more precisely in the fact that knowledge has not grasped the being of reason in and for itself. This is infinite, however, only insofar as it is absolute freedom, and thus presupposes itself as the immediate determinacy of its knowledge. It thereby reduces itself to finitude, and appears as the eternal movement of suspending this immediacy and comprehending itself

The progress of the spirit is development, because its existing phase, knowledge, involves consciousness in and for itself as the purpose or rationale. Thus the action of translating this purpose into reality is strictly only this formal transition into manifestation. Insofar as knowledge is infinite negativity, this translation in the concept is creativity in general. Insofar as knowledge is only abstract or formal, the spirit in it does not conform to its concept, and its purpose is to bring forth the absolute fulfilment and the absolute freedom of its knowledge.

The way of the spirit is: (a) to be theoretical: it has to do with its immediate determinacy and the positing of this determinacy as its own; -- or, it has to free knowledge from its presuppositions and therefore from its abstractions, and make the determinacy subjective. Since the knowledge in itself is determined in and for itself or exists as free intelligence, it is immediately: (b) will, practical spirit, which in the first place is immediately willed, and its determination of will is to be freed from its subjectivity, so that it exists as free will and objective spirit.

The theoretical and the practical spirit still fall in the sphere of the subjective spirit in general; this knowledge and will are still formal. But as spirit it is above all the unity of subjectivity and objectivity. As subjective spirit it is thus just as productive, though its productions are primarily formal. The production of the theoretical spirit is only of its ideal world, whereas the production of the practical spirit is of formal material and the content of its own world.

The doctrine of the spirit is usually treated as empirical psychology, with the spirit considered as a collection of powers and faculties which find themselves thrown together in a coincidental fashion. Thus it seems that one or the other faculty could just as well exist or not, a view which does not occur in physics, for example, where it is clear that nature would lose quite a bit if such a feature as magnetism did not exist. -- The relation of the faculties to each other is of course seen as extremely necessary or purposeful, but this utility of the faculties appears often to be very remote, or even at times in bad taste.

Psychology belongs, like logic, among those sciences which in modern times have derived the least use from the more general intellectual culture and the deeper concepts of reason. It thus finds itself in a dreadful condition. To be sure, the turn taken by Kantian philosophy has given it greater importance: it has even been claimed that in its empirical condition it constitutes the foundation of metaphysics, for metaphysics is to consist of nothing but the empirical apprehension and the analysis of the facts of human consciousness, above all as facts, just as they are given. But this view of psychology, which mixes the standpoint of consciousness with anthropology, has actually changed nothing of its condition. It has only meant that, both for the spirit as such and for metaphysics and philosophy generally, all attempts to recognise the necessity of what is in and for itself have been abandoned, along with the effort to realise the concept and the truth.

(a.) Theoretical Spirit

Intelligence finds itself determined; as knowledge, however, intelligence consists in treating what is found as its own. Its activity is to be reason for itself because it is reason in itself and to make subjective its objectivity subsisting in and for itself Intelligence is therefore not receptive, but rather essentially active, suspending the pretence of finding reason, or raising the purely formal knowledge, which it is as the self-discovery of reason, to a determinate knowledge of itself The manner of this elevation is itself rational, because it is reason, and a necessary, conceptually determined transition of one determination of its activity into the other.

(I) The distinction of intelligence from will is often incorrectly taken to mean that each has a fixed and separate existence, as if will could exist without intelligence, or the activity of intelligence could be without will. But this would miss the truth of the will, for only free self-determination is will, as the will is intelligence, and freedom itself exists only as self-certainty in the immediate determination subsisting in itself Thus the truth of intelligence manifests itself as will, or rather, intelligence shows itself in the will as truth. The will of the spirit to be intelligence is its self-determination, by which the purposes and interests posited by the spirit are abstracted so that it does not relate to itself as will.

The most trivial form of that false distinction is the imagined possibility that the understanding could exist without the heart, and the heart without the understanding. Such a view is the abstraction of the observant understanding, which holds fast to such distinctions. just as it is the actual understanding in the individual which makes this kind of separation, ushers in the untruth of intellectual thought and remains fixed there, thus it is an understanding which is just as much will. But it is not philosophy which should take such untruths of thought and the imagination for truth.-A number of other phrases used for intelligence, namely, that it receives and accepts impressions from outside, that ideas arise through the causal operations of external things upon it, and so on, belong to a point of view which mixes sensory and rational determinations, a standpoint that is alien to the spirit and earn less appropriate for philosophy.-That the intelligence appears determined in infinitely multiple, contingent ways is equally the standpoint of entirely finite individuality, and the extreme untruth of empirical observation.

(2) A favourite form of reflection deals with forces and faculties of the soul, the intelligence, or the spirit. In regards to a faculty-the dynamics of Aristotle have an entirely different meaning-it characterises being for itself and is different from the entelechy, from the activity of being for itself and from reality. Faculty, like force, is the fixed determinacy of any thought content, conceived as reflection into self Force is, to be sure, the infinity of form, of inside and outside; but its essential finitude constitutes the indifference of the content in contrast to the form (ibid. note). In this lies the irrational element which by this form of reflection and observation of the spirit, treating the spirit as a number of forces, is brought into the spirit as it is also brought into nature. What can be distinguished in this activity is stereotyped as an independent determinacy, and the spirit is made in this way into a skeleton-like, mechanical collection. If a force of the spirit, that is, its contents, the particular determinacy which it contains, is considered, it proves again to be determinate, that is, dialectic and transitory, not independent. Thus it is precisely the used form of a force that suspends itself which should be the reflection into self or determinacy, and is affixed to independence. In this way the concept emerges, in which the forces disappear.

This concept and the dialectic are intelligence itself pure subjectivity of the self in which the determinations as fluid moments are suspended, and for which the absolute concrete is the night of the self where there is intelligence as well as the determinations of their activity which are taken as forces. As the simple identity of this multiplicity it determines itself as the simplicity of a determinacy, understanding, the form of a force, of an isolated activity, and grasps itself as intuition, the power of imagination, the faculty of understanding, and so on. But this isolation, the abstractions of activities and the opinions of them are not the concept and the rational truth themselves.

As the soul, intelligence is immediately determined, as consciousness it is related to this determinacy as to an external object; as intelligence it finds itself thus determined. It is therefore: (1) feeling, the inarticulate weave of the spirit into itself in which it is to some extent palpable, and contains the whole material of its knowledge. For the sake of the immediacy in which the spirit is as feeling or sensation, it exists above all only as individual and subjective.

The form of sensation is, to be sure, a determinate affection, but this determinacy is simple and in it the differentiation of both their content against other contents, and the externality of it against the subjectivity which is still not posited.

It is commonly enough assumed that the spirit has in its sensation the material of its representations, but this thesis is more usually understood in a sense antithetical to that which it has here. In contrast with the simplicity of feeling, it is usual rather to assume that the primary mental phase is judgment generally and the distinction of consciousness into subject and object, and the particular quality of sensation is derived from an independent object, external or internal. Here in the sphere of the spirit, this standpoint of consciousness opposed to idealism has been submerged. The feeling or the sensation are, by their form, resembling content, since it is this immediate, still implicitly undifferentiated, dull knowledge of the spirit.

Aristotle, too, recognised the determination of sensation, for he saw that the sentient subject and the sensed object, separated by consciousness, only exist as the sensation of the possibility, though he said of the sensation that the entelechy of the sentient and the sensed are one and the same.-No prejudice is probably more false than the thesis that nothing exists in thought which does not exist in the senses, --and indeed, in the usual sense which is attributed to Aristotle. His actual philosophy, however, is the exact opposite of this idea.

Another equally familiar prejudice as this historical one is the idea that there is more in feeling than in thought; this point is often made in regards to moral and religious feelings. Now it has happened that the material which itself is the feeling spirit is the being determined in and for itself of reason. But this form of simplicity is the lowest an the worst, in which it can not be as spirit, as the free entity or the infinite generality which is its essence. It must, rather, above all go beyond this untrue manner of its being, because it exists in immediacy as determinate, and in any case is only a contingent, subjective, and particular entity. If someone refers on any topic not to the nature and the concept of the issue, least of all to reasons or to the generalities of common sense, but to one's own feeling, the only thing to do is to leave them alone, because by their behaviour they reject the community of rationality, and shut themselves up in their own isolated subjectivity, their private and particular selves.

The abstract identical direction of the spirit in sensation, as in all other of its further determinations, is attention: the moment of the formal self-determination of the intelligence.

This self-determination is, however, essentially not abstract; as an infinitude it dissolves the simplicity of its determinate being and thereby suspends its immediacy. Thus it posits itself as a negative, the felt entity, distinct from the intelligence as reflective into itself and from the subject, in which feeling is suspended. This level of reflection is the representation.

(2) The representing activity of the intelligence is: (a) recollection. With its simple, dissolving sensation and its determination as a negative extreme set against the reflection into itself recollection posits the content of the sensation as

subsisting outside of itself Thus it throws content into space and time, and is intuitive. The intuition is immediate, insofar as the abstract alienation and the intelligence are not all reflection into themselves and set against this externality.

This positing, however, is the other extreme of the diremption: the intelligence posits the content of its feeling in its own inwardness, in a space and time of its own. In this way the content is an image or representation in general, freed from its initial immediacy and abstract individuality among other things, and taken up, at first abstractly and ideally, into the form of the self's generality.

Recollection is the relation of both, the subsumption of the immediate, individual intuition under this formal generality, the representation which is the same content. Thus the intelligence in the determinate sensation and its intuition are inward, recognise themselves thus, no longer require the intuition and possess it as their own.

(b) The intelligence which is active in this possession is the reproductive imagination, the production of images from the inferiority of the self The concrete images are in the first place related to the external, immediate space and time which are treasured along with them.-But since the image in the subject, where it is treasured, only has the negative unity in which it is carried and receives its concretion, thus its originally concrete condition, by which as a unit of sensation and intuition or in consciousness it is determined, has been broken up. The reproduced content, belonging as it does to the self-identical unity of the intelligence, and emerging from its interior into the representation, is a general representation, which supplies the link of association for the images which according to circumstances are either more abstract or more concrete representations.

The "laws of the association of idea? were of great interest, especially during that outburst of empirical psychology which occurred at the same time as the decline of philosophy. In the first place, it is not "ideas' which are associated. Secondly, these modes of association are not laws, just for the reason that there are so many laws about the same thing that they suggest an arbitrariness and a contingency which are the very opposite of a law. The ongoing sequence of images and representations suggested by association is in general the play of thoughtless representation, in which the determination of the intelligence is still an entirely formal generality, a content given in the images.- Image and idea are only distinguished by the fact that the former is more concrete; representation, the content, may be an image, concept, or idea, but always has the character, though belonging to intelligence, of being given and immediate in terms of its content.-Otherwise it appears, since intuition is immediate relation, the self an ideal one, and thus its self-reflection is an external generality, which is not yet the determination of the content, whereas representation and its production are a determinate generality-that intuition, representation, and imagination are essentially thinking, although they are not yet liberated thought, and their content is not a thought. --

Abstraction, which occurs in the representative activity, by which general representations are produced, is frequently explained as the incidence of many similar images one upon the other, and is supposed to be thus made intelligible. If this superimposition is to be no mere accident or without principle, a force of attraction in similar images must be assumed, or something of the sort, which at the same time would have the negative power of rubbing off the still-dissimilar elements against each other. This force is in fact intelligence itself the self as a general entity that by its memory gives the images generality directly.

Thus even the association of representations is a subsumption of the individual under a single generality. This generality is at first a form of the intelligence. But it is in itself just as much determinate, concrete subjectivity, and its own content can be a thought, concept, or idea. As the subsumption of images under a specific content, intelligence recollects them in themselves as determinate, and forms them into their content. In this way it is creative imagination, imagination which symbolises, allegorises, or poeticises.

Intelligence has been so far perfected in the determinate recollection of creative imagination that its self-generated content has a pictorial existence. Yet the material of the pictorial creation is given, and the product does not have the immediacy of existence. Intelligence must give the creation this immediacy: as intelligence in the creation forms the totality of the representation, it has turned back from its particularisation in subjective representation and animal intuition to the free, identical relation to itself This recollection of the intuition is memory.

(c) Memory (Mnemosyne, muse) is the unity of the independent representation and the intuition, with the former as a free attempt to utter itself immediately.-This immediacy is, because the intelligence is not yet practical, immediate, or given; but in this identity the intuition does not count positively or as self-representing, but as a representative of something else. It is an image, which has received as its soul and meaning an independent representation of the intelligence. This intuition is the sign.

The sign is any immediate intuition, but representing a totally different content from what it has for itself;-it is the pyramid, into which a foreign soul is conveyed and preserved. The sign is different from the symbol, an intuition which according to its essence and concept is determined to be more or less the thought which it expresses as symbol. Intelligence, therefore, gives proof of a freer choice and authority in the use of intuitions when it treats them as signifying rather than symbolic.

Usually, language and the sign are relegated somewhere into the appendix on psychology, or even logic, with no recognition of their necessity and connection in the system of intelligent activity. The true place for the sign is the one just mentioned: where intelligence, which intuitively generates time and place, now gives its own independent representations a determinate existence, a filled place and time, treating the intuition which it has as its own material of sensation, eliminating its immediate and unique representation, and giving it another as its meaning and soul.-This sign-creating activity may justifiably be called memory, or "productive memory," since memory, which is often used in ordinary life as interchangeable and synonymous with recollection, and even with representation and imagination, above all has only to do with signs. And even if it is used in this more precise sense, it is otherwise thought of as only the reproductive memory: the intelligence essentially produces, however, what it reproduces.

The intuition, which is used for a sign is in its immediate phase given and spatial. But since it exists only as suspended, and the intelligence is its negativity, the true form of the intuition as a sign is its existence in time, -- but this existence vanishes in the moment of being, and its tone is the fulfilled manifestation of its self-proclaimed inferiority. The tone which articulates itself further to express specific representations -- speech and its system, language -- gives to sensations and intuitions a second and higher existence than they immediately possess, and invests the images with existence in the realm of representation.

The identity of intuition in the sign and its meaning is primarily a single production; but as a unity with the intelligence it is just as essentially general. 'Me activity of recollecting this and thereby making it general, as well as reproducing it, is the outwardly retentive and reproductive memory.

There are many signs in general, and as such they are absolutely contingent in juxtaposition to each other. The empty bind which fixes such sequences and holds them in this order is the entirely abstract, pure power of subjectivity, -- the memory, which is called mechanical for the complete externality in which the members of such sequences are juxtaposed.

The name is thus the thing, as it exists and has validity in the realm of representation. But it also has an externality brought forth from the intelligence, and it is the intuition which is inessential for itself standing in the use of intelligence and subjectively made, so that it only has value through the meaning given to it by the intelligence, which is the determinate representation in and for itself and the thing or the objective entity. Mechanical memory is the formal suspension of that subjectivity, whereby the contradiction of the sign falls away and the intelligence makes itself for itself in the habit of language a thing, as an immediate objectivity. In this way, through the memory, it makes the transition to thought.

(3) Through the recollection of its immediate determinacy and the manifestation of its subjective activity of determination, the unity and truth of intelligence are achieved: the thought. The thought is the thing, the simple identity of subjective and objective. What is thought, is; and what is, is only insofar as it is thought.

Thought is in the first place formal: generality as generality, and just as much being as the simple subjectivity of intelligence. In this way it is not determinate in and for itself; the recollected representations brought to thought are, insofar as they are still content, -- a content which in itself is only the determinate being in and for itself of reason.

Thought, however, as the free generality which it is only as pure negativity, is therefore not: (a) only the formally identical understanding, but (b) essentially diremption and determination, -- judgment, and (c) the identity which finds itself in this particularisation, the concept and reason. Intelligence has determinate being in comprehension, though it existed at first as immediate material, and in itself it is absolutely only its own, thereby it exists not as determinate being, but as the act of determination.

In logic there is thought, in the first place as it is in itself then as it is for itself and in and for itself-these have been viewed as being, reflection, concept, and as idea. In the soul it is alert self-possession; in consciousness it also occurs as a phase. Thought thus recurs again and again in these different parts of philosophy, because they are different only through the element and the form of the antithesis they are in, but thought is this one and the same centre, to which as to their truth the antitheses return.

Thought, as the free concept, is also free in terms of the content.. The determinacy of reason is the proper determinacy of subjective intelligence, and as determinate it is its content and existence. Thinking subjectivity is thereby actual; its determinations are purposes; it is free will.

(b.) Practical Spirit

The spirit as intelligence is primarily, however, abstract for itself; as free will it is fulfilled, because it exists as concept, as self-determining. This fulfilled being for itself or individuality constitutes the side of existence or reality, the idea of the spirit, whose concept is reason.

This existence of the self-determination of spirit is in the first place immediate, where spirit finds itself and as inward in itself or through nature it is self-determining individuality. It is therefore: (1) practical feeling.

Free will is the individuality or the pure negativity of the self-determining being for itself which is simply identical with reason and therefore general subjectivity itself, the will as intelligence. The immediate individuality of the will in practical feelings thus has this content, but as immediately individual, hence contingent and subjective.

An appeal is sometimes made to the feeling of right and morality which the person has in himself to his benevolent dispositions and so on, and to his heart in general, that is, to the subject, insofar as the different practical feelings are all united in it. As far as this appeal implies: (1) that these determinations are immanent in themselves, and (2) that when feeling is opposed to the logical understanding, it, and not the partial abstractions of the understanding, may be the totality, the appeal has a legitimate meaning. But on the other hand, feeling too may be one-sided, inessential, and bad; through the form of the immediacy it is essentially contingent and subjective. The rational, which exists in the shape of rationality when it is apprehended by thought, has the same content as the practical feeling has, but depicted in its generality and necessity, in its objectivity and truth.

Thus it is foolish, on the one hand, to suppose that in the transition from feeling to law and duty there is any loss of content and excellence; it is this transition which first brings feeling to its truth. It is equally foolish to consider intellect as superfluous or even harmful to feeling, heart, and will; the truth and, what is the same thing, the rationality of the heart and will can only find a place in the generality of the intelligence, not in the individuality of feeling.

On the other hand, however, it is suspicious and even worse to cling to feelings and the heart as against intelligent rationality, because all that the former holds more than the latter is only particular subjectivity, vanity and caprice.-For the same reason it is out of place in an observation of feelings to deal with anything beyond their form and to discuss their content; for the latter, when thought, is precisely what constitutes the self-determinations of the spirit in its generality and necessity, its rights and duties.

The practical feeling, as the self-determination of the thinking subject in general, contains the "ought" in relation to its subsisting individuality, which is in itself worth nothing, and is determinate only in its identity with generality as a true being subsisting for itself But the practical feeling, in its immediate individuality with the "ought," exists only in relation to determinacy; and since in this immediacy it still has no necessary identity, it only yields the feeling of pleasantness or unpleasantness.

(1) Delight, joy, pain, and so on, shame, repentance, contentment, and so on, are partly only modifications of the formal practical feeling in general, but also partly different in the content which constitutes the determinacy of their "ought."

(2) The celebrated question of the origin of evil in the world, at least insofar as evil is understood merely as unpleasantness and pain, finds its answer here. For evil is nothing other than the incongruity between the "is" and the "ought." This "ought," however, has many meanings, indeed, infinitely many, since contingent purposes also have the form of the "ought." In the case of these casual aims, evil only practices what is rightfully due to their vanity-and nullity. They are themselves the evil, and that there are such and numerous other individuals inadequate to the idea derives from the necessary indifference of the concept towards immediate being in general: the concept, as

free reality, relates to being essentially as determinate nullity in itself although being is also given access to free reality through the concept;-a contradiction which is called evil. In death there is neither evil nor pain; for in inorganic nature the concept does not confront its existence. But in life, and still more in the spirit, there. is this distinction at hand, and this negativity, activity, self freedom, are the principles of evil and of pain. --Jacob Boehme viewed serfhood as pain and torture, and as the source of nature and the spirit.

The practical "ought" is (2) a real judgment. The immediacy of feeling is, for the self-determination of the will, a negation; it thus constitutes the subjectivity of the will, which should be suspended in order for the will to be identical for itself Since this activity of the form is not yet liberated and is therefore formal, the will is still natural will, drive and inclination, and with the more precise determinacy that the totality of the practical spirit places itself into an individual one of the limited determinations, namely, passion.

Inclinations and passions have as their contents the same self-determinations as the practical feelings. Because the ones, like the others, are immediate self-determinations which do not yet have the form of rationality, they are multiple particularities. They have, on the one hand, the rational nature of the spirit as their basis, but on the other hand they belong to the subjective, individual will; they are thus essentially infected by contingency, and stand to the individual and to each other in a relation marked by external, confining necessity.

The same holds for the inclinations as for the feelings: although they are self-determinations of the free will in itself in terms ' of content they are not free for themselves, nor have they reached generality and objectivity. To be sure, passion already contains this in its determination, though it is limited to a particularity of the will and the subjectivity of the individual, be the content what it may. But with regard to the inclinations the question is raised: which are good, and which are bad; up to what degree will the good continue to be good; and, as there are many, each with its own particularities, how have they, since they are after all located within one subject and according to experience can not all be gratified, suffered at least a little reciprocal restriction? In the first place, as regards these many drives and inclinations, the case is much the same as with the psychic forces, the aggregate of which is the theoretical spirit,-a collection which is now increased by the number of drives. The formal rationality of the drive and the inclination consists merely in the general drive not to be subjective, but rather to be realised. Yet their true rationality can not reveal itself from a perspective of external reflection, partly because it presupposes that a number of independent natural determinations and immediate drives are fixed, partly because the immanent reflection of spirit itself goes beyond their particularity and immediacy, and gives them a rationality and objectivity in which they exist as necessary relations, rights, and duties. It is this objectification which reveals their content, their relation to each other, and above all their truth. As Plato showed, the full reality of justice can only be presented in the objective figure of justice, namely, the construction of the state as ethical life.

The answer to the question, then, of which are the good and rational inclinations, and how they are to be subordinated to each other, transforms itself into the exposition of the laws and forms of common life produced by the relations of the spirit as it suspends its subjectivity and realises itself,-- an objectivity in which precisely its self-determinations in general lose the form of inclinations, just as the content loses subjectivity, contingency, or caprice.

The general moment in these drives is the individual subject, the act of satisfying impulses or formal rationality, namely, the translation from subjectivity into objectivity. In the latter the former returns to itself: that the thing which has emerged contains the moment of subjective individuality, is called the interest.-- Since the activity is the individual subjectivity in that dialectical movement, nothing is brought about without interest.

Here, however, interest does not yet exist as the merely formal activity or pure subjectivity, but has as drive or inclination a determinate content from the immediate will. The dialectic of this multiple and particular content is, however, the simple subjectivity of the will itself which raises the contradiction of the drives in the first place as reflecting will into formal generality, and itself makes (3) happiness its goal.

Happiness is the confused representation of the satisfaction of all drives, which, however, are either entirely or partly sacrificed to each other, preferred and presupposed. Their mutual limitation, on the one hand, is a mixture of qualitative and quantitative determinations; on the other hand, since the inclination is a subjective and immediate basis for determination, it is the subjective feeling and good pleasure which must have the decisive vote as to where happiness is to be placed.

The will, which as passion is abstract understanding and converges into a unity of its determinacies, is liberated in the general purpose of happiness from this individualisation. The many particular inclinations, however, still taken as immediate, independent determinations, are at the same time suspended in the unity of purpose of happiness, and as such are dependent. The will stands as this indeterminate generality, reflected into itself over the individual inclination; the generality is initially that of the will, since the two converge and thereby produce determinate individuality and reality; the will exists from the standpoint of having to choose between inclinations, and involves choice.

The will is in this way free for itself since it is, as the negativity of its immediate determinate being, reflected into itself; however, insofar as the content that it includes with this individuality and reality remains a particularity, it is only real as subjective and contingent will. As the contradiction of realising itself in particularity and yet finding satisfaction in the generality from which it at the same time derives, the will is in the first place the process of dispersion and the suspension of an inclination through the other, and the partial gratification which it entails, through another to infinity.

The truth, however, of the particular aim of the will, of the particularity which is just as much determinate as suspended, and of the abstract individuality, of choice, which yields just as much of a content in such a purpose as it does not yield, is the unity in which both are only a moment; the absolute individuality of the will, its pure freedom, which determines itself for itself in and for itself The spirit in this truth of self-determination, which is itself the goal as the pure reflection into itself is thus, as general, objective will, the objective spirit.

www.ingramcontent.com/pod-product-compliance
Lightning Source LLC
Chambersburg PA
CBHW060502110426
42738CB00055B/2590